# CHURCHILL,
# KITCHENER AND
# LLOYD GEORGE

# CHURCHILL, KITCHENER AND LLOYD GEORGE

## FIRST WORLD WARLORDS

### STEPHEN CLIFFE

FONTHILL

*For Amy, born on the 11th of November, and Allan,*
*named for a brave young soldier killed on the Somme*

Fonthill Media Limited
www.fonthillmedia.com
office@fonthillmedia.com

First published in the United Kingdom 2014

British Library Cataloguing in Publication Data:
A catalogue record for this book is available from the British Library

ISBN 978-1-78155-272-8

Typeset in 10pt on 13 pt Sabon
Printed and bound by CPI Group (UK) Ltd, Croydon, CR0 4YY

# Contents

# Acknowledgements

I wish to acknowledge those admirable men and women of the late Edwardian era and their unyielding vigour in the face of adversity. My thanks also go to Coral Dranfield for her invaluable suggestions and criticism in reading my drafts, and to Amanda Cliffe for permitting the use of her photo of Allan Cliffe.

# Introduction

*Even when your troops are in the most desperate straits,*
*They will have no fear,*
*And with nowhere else to turn,*
*They will stand firm.*
Sun-Tzu, *The Art of War* (sixth century BC)

When the jingling, freshly kitted British Expeditionary Force crossed to France in the late summer of 1914, it was Britain's most professional army since Wellington's battle-seasoned Peninsular army of veterans had pursued the retreating soldiers of Napoleon out of Spain and over the Pyrenees a century before. The BEF contained many officers and men with comparatively recent professional experience in the South African War. It was a small army, but very tough, polished and highly trained.

Disembarkation at the port of Le Havre was effected with smooth efficiency by the Royal Navy, still the world's strongest naval fleet and in total command of the Channel, despite the potential threat of the German High Seas Fleet bottled up in its northern ports by British blockade and the minuscule numbers of U-boats then available to Germany's admirals. The planning for this smooth transition from peace to war, the mobilisation of thousands of men, and the rapid gathering and movement of mountains of food, equipment and munitions to the right place at the right time was due largely to the hard work and knowledge of two men. One of these was a comparatively obscure politician and lawyer, Lord Haldane, forgotten except as a mere footnote in history, whose hard work at the War Office in preparation for such an emergency was now bearing fruit, even though its author, known for his admiration of German efficiency, was regarded as too pro-German to be trusted with a key wartime office in the anti-Teutonic hysteria then prevailing. The other was a hero of the people and icon of Empire, lionised the world over as the supreme incarnation of a peculiarly British warlord then in vogue—the strong, silent man—Lord Kitchener of Khartoum, he of the luxuriant moustache, peremptory pointing finger and imperious staring eyes; 'The greatest recruiting poster of all time!'

Famously, he had avenged that romantic Victorian figure of legend, General Gordon. He did it by a careful, meticulous progress across the unforgiving deserts of Egypt and the Sudan, with a small army, composed mainly of Egyptian troops stiffened by British regular army units, the construction of a 235-mile military railway, and Royal Navy gunboats on the Nile. His scientifically placed Maxim guns and artillery had decimated and crushed the vastly superior numbers of the wild Dervish army. In that battle at Omdurman, a young lieutenant, Winston Churchill of the 21st Lancers, took part in one of the last cavalry charges of the British Army.

Now, twenty years later, the two were colleagues in a Liberal wartime government, Kitchener as the newly appointed Minister for War, still with the rank of field marshal, and Churchill, a mere major in the Oxfordshire Yeomanry, a local militia regiment, but a senior political figure as First Lord of the Admiralty, the effective civilian head of the Navy.

Kitchener, a diligent worker and planner but with a rather chaotic administrative style, had plunged into his task at the outbreak of war in August, earning admiration from the enemy. General Ludendorff wrote:

> He created armies out of next to nothing, trained and equipped them. Through his genius alone, England developed side by side with France, into an opponent capable of meeting Germany on even terms whereby the position on the front in France in 1915 was so seriously changed to Germany's disadvantage.

The German war plan of violating Belgian neutrality and bypassing the heavily defended French fortresses to turn their northern flank was effectively blocked by the sudden and unexpected appearance of the BEF. The highly trained infantry put up such fast and well-directed rifle fire into the Germans that they believed the British must be using large numbers of machine guns. In fact, Kitchener had not yet been able to provide these in any number, and it would be some months, even years, into the war before munitions production was on a wartime footing. Kitchener's name seemed an amulet of success, a good luck token that had extracted victory and peace from the débâcle of the South African War a decade before against the plucky little Boer republics. Here he was again, fresh from his recent reorganisation of the vast Indian Army, about to perform one of those miracles that Britons had come to expect from their tall, stern, steely-eyed hero. But was he past his best?

There is little doubt that without him the war would have got off to a faltering start, but Kitchener was not destined to complete the task. Supreme warlord and commanding personality though he was, other men were to take up the reins from his cold, dead hands. Though his warlike colleague at the Admiralty, Winston Churchill, rose to this supreme role nearly thirty years later, when he was almost Kitchener's age, his was not to be the guiding hand on the careering carriage of state at this time of crisis. That lot fell to a combative little Welshman, a Liberal radical, watered-down Welsh nationalist and country lawyer, now reborn as an international statesman and would-be saviour of the nation. Lloyd George fumed during the crisis, until the overwhelmed Prime Minister, Asquith, an Oxford intellectual, reluctantly let him into the War Office, then, outmanoeuvred by political combinations, was pushed aside, vacating the prime ministerial chair itself, and finally allowing the dynamic driving force of the Welsh Wizard full rein. He seized those reins and lashed up the horses into an effort no one thought possible. Britain became a war machine.

It was a bumpy ride, and at one of the twists and turns called 'Dardanelles', Churchill was flung off and found himself floundering with a battalion in the mud and blood of the trenches. But Lloyd George had his eye on him (and an eye to the main chance) and picked him up again as soon as he decently could. Churchill had lost the Admiralty, but he eventually gained the War Ministry. Like Lloyd George, one day he too would be an historic wartime prime minister, but he would be remembered for far longer, and with a lustre about his name that the Welsh radical, brilliant as he was, never fully attained, though he well deserved it. Theirs was one of the most significant political partnerships in history (bearing in mind that there are no friendships in politics at this level).

Each has been described as the greatest leader that Britain ever had in the twentieth century. And many forget that Churchill had a political life as potentially glittering during and after the Great War as a relatively young man, long before his glory days in the Second World War. He was very much the junior partner when teamed with Lloyd George, but almost a dangerously dynamic force. These three, Churchill, Kitchener, and Lloyd George, were without doubt Britain's first world warlords of a vanished Imperial age. They were all men of phenomenal energy, compulsive social interactors at the top level, making their own opportunities to exercise their talents and gratify their colossal ambitions. They were realists but romantic, pragmatists but idealistic, and they did what few politicians today seem to want to do—they looked unpleasant facts in the face and did something about it. Without them, the world we live in today would be a rather different place. For Churchill, this was his apprenticeship in the management of war, which was to be of such great advantage to his country in the re-run.

In this book I take the reader on a brisk canter through the events leading up to the outbreak of the Great War, introducing these powerful leading personalities and describing their relationships with one another, which, for good or ill, shaped the lives of millions and guided the momentous conflict that decided the fate of Europe. Limitation of space has meant that the action is condensed to a mainly Western Front perspective. Consequently, the Russians, whose early contribution was so important, are barely mentioned.

Born in 1953, during Churchill's second and final premiership, I am just old enough to remember some of the men and women who lived through the Armageddon of the First World War. In my childhood 'The War' meant the Second World War, as to a certain extent it still does. That was the modern war of our parents, not the 'old-fashioned' predecessor of our grandparents' lives, although we understood that it was a very big and dreadful war. As a young reporter on a local paper in the 1970s, I occasionally interviewed old men who described their time in the trenches and at campaigns and battles with the ominous names of Gallipoli, The Somme, Ypres and the like. I asked one genial old chap how he could return to normality at the mill after all that. He replied simply, 'You just remember the good times.' Almost every family in Britain had someone in those places at those times. It is strange, a century on, to see those young men in khaki come marching back out of the dim mists of a Flanders past.

*Steve Cliffe, 2014*

# 1

# Goat-footed Syren

*This extraordinary figure of our time, this syren, this goat-footed*
*bard, this half human visitor to our age from the hag-ridden*
*magic and enchanted woods of Celtic antiquity.*
J. M. Keynes

The man to whom Churchill was politically apprenticed, and to whom Kitchener was largely indebted for the successful completion of his work, was born in 1863 in a grimy terraced street in the smoky, working class, Manchester inner-city suburb of Chorlton on Medlock. Churchill, of course, was born in the ducal surroundings of Blenheim Palace, and Kitchener in a villa in Ireland.

David Lloyd George's father William was a schoolmaster, his mother Elizabeth had been a servant, and their humble abode was typical of the early married life of a lower middle class couple striving to get on in the world. Like many Welshmen before and since, William George could not get on with the English, and particularly with the working class governors of his Lancashire school. 'I would rather give orders to them than receive them,' he said. His health was not good, and the foul atmosphere of a heavily industrial area aided the couple's decision to return to William's native Pembrokeshire to try their hand at farming—his family background. Alas, it did not help. William died of pneumonia when David was barely eighteen months old.

A telegram, short and simple in its pathos—'Richard come'—was dispatched to Richard Lloyd, Elizabeth's brother in Carnarvonshire, the village shoemaker, a devout Baptist preacher, who immediately complied. Elizabeth, David and his elder sister, Mary Ellen, were carried off to the romantic windswept shores of Tremadoc Bay, which with its wooded and mountainous hinterland was to be forever associated with the career of its illustrious adopted son. Within a few months, another son, named William after his father, was born posthumously.

At 'Highgate', a small cottage built of large boulders adjoining the cobbler's shop in the village of Llanystumdwy, the little family settled down to a simple life. David, William and Mary Ellen entered the village school, an Anglican establishment, where David was superbly taught by the schoolmaster David Evans but later jibbed against the conventional religious teachings of the school. His 'Uncle Lloyd', as

Richard came to be called, was always over-fond of his nephew, remarking once while watching him haranguing a small group of other children and underlining his arguments by striking the iron railings with a stick, 'Mark my words, that boy will be somebody one day!'

David made quick progress at the school that he attended from the age of four, being particularly good at mathematics. He was said to be a bit of a bookworm, encouraged by his Uncle Lloyd's bookish interests. Not only was Richard a lay preacher at a local chapel but he had radical views, and the shoemaker's workshop was a gathering ground for discussion, known as the 'village parliament', where David listened to wide-ranging debates, noting the differing oratorical styles. He was also lucky that David Evans had a dramatic ability to capture the children's interest with a thrilling narrative technique. The schoolmaster was a sound scholar who took the time to give his star pupils, including David, very personal attention and tuition.

Lloyd George once jokingly remarked that he first realised he was 'a genius' when as a boy he found himself reading the geometric principles of Euclid in the topmost boughs of an oak tree. 'What an extraordinary fellow I am!' he had exclaimed to himself. By the standards of Llanystumdwy, he certainly was. It was at about this time that another less pleasant revelation occurred to the young David. He was baptised at the age of twelve by Uncle Lloyd in the little stream which ran beside the Penymaes Chapel, in accordance with the precept that such matters should be deferred until the child reached an age of understanding. Many years later, Lloyd George confessed to his mistress, Frances Stevenson, that the following night the disagreeable notion flashed upon him that there 'may not be truth in any of it' and he leapt out of bed in the darkness with an anguished yelp of astonishment.

An incident at the local school also revealed the ruthless streak in David at an early age. His brother William confided in old age, 'David was a very naughty boy, and always getting into trouble,' and that he, William, often had to shield him from the consequences of his actions. One such was a revolt David staged by bullying the other pupils into refusing to recite the Creed before the parson and gentry of the Anglican school board for their annual visit. The poor headmaster was made to look a fool before his guests, until William, feeling the injustice of the popular schoolmaster's plight and perhaps fearing his brother less than most of the other pupils, broke the silence and began with 'I believe' and the rest joined in, except David, who was striking a blow for Welsh radicalism and nonconformity. And it had a result—never again were the children, mostly of nonconformist parents, required to recite the Anglican Creed or Catechism in public. William, however, got a thumping.

That this radicalism was imbibed by David from his Uncle Lloyd cannot be doubted. The man heaped his eldest nephew with praise on every occasion, and his letters to Lloyd George when he was an influential politician continued to exert some influence on the actions of the young MP. It has been said that Lloyd George became the first 'cottage-bred' Prime Minister. If so, he did it from a position of privilege within his native community. The 'Lloyds' were well-to-do by comparison with most families and Uncle Lloyd employed several hands in his workshop, supplying footwear to farms for miles around. He was also a respected lay preacher of impeccable moral standing. David's quietly spoken mother Elizabeth was also a proud woman. She would not allow her son to join the other village children on garden weeding expeditions, despite the lure of the odd sixpence in reward. But he was a popular lad, whose companionship was sought after, and he struck a further blow for Welsh freedom by secretly leading poaching (mainly fishing) expeditions on the estates of the local Tory squire, Ellis-Nanney.

Although in later years Lloyd George privately spoke of the 'terrible boredom' of his childhood, and brother William complained that they had to walk to chapel and back three times on a Sunday wearing antiquated clothes, the flavour of the village left a lasting mark upon his imagination. Llanystumdwy is still beautifully situated, with its old stone bridge athwart the little River Dwyfor, a swift-flowing mountain stream that tumbles down a brief ten miles from the hills, then debouches into the sea a mile from the village. The river plunges through a series of deep crystal pools, rushing over massive glacial boulders, its banks embowered by those magical Celtic woods, remarkable even by Welsh standards, mentioned by Keynes. Were Lloyd George an insensitive lad, he could hardly have failed to be moved by the moods of such primordial surroundings. The rural symbolism of his childhood figured again and again in speeches by the famous politician. Thus we have his oratorical descriptions of suddenly changing light, from darkly morose to a brilliant illuminating sunshine, a wind that stirred the topmost branches of the trees like a hopeful sigh, and glimpses of the distant mountains, the broad sunny uplands that held the promise of a wider world to the aspirant young radical.

Lloyd George may have wanted to escape, and did escape, from Llanystumdwy— but he always came back again, bringing a succession of politicians, newspapermen, academics and literary figures to view the origins of the 'cottage-bred' Prime Minister, perhaps as an explanation of himself as a phenomenon, the silver-tongued orator and goat-footed bard who could 'charm the birds from the trees'. It was partly hype, but some of it was true. Certainly, at the end of his long life he returned to die in the village, and his bones lie in the Celtic woods above the tumbling river, beneath a boulder chosen by himself, from which he had fished as a boy.

That, however, lay far in the future. The immediate future beckoned with exciting possibilities. First of all, David was offered a post as student teacher at the village school, but rejected the profession of his father in favour of one with greater potential for public exposure, opting to pursue a career in the law. Perhaps the large picture of Abraham Lincoln placed prominently in the Lloyd George household had influenced his choice. Uncle Lloyd and Lloyd George both idolised the great American lawyer, politician and fellow Baptist, who had helped abolish slavery and fought a war to defend his principles. Uncle Lloyd's contacts introduced David to a firm of solicitors with a practice at Portmadoc, a bustling slate port a few miles along the coast, and he began working there in summer 1878. The following year he was accepted as an articled clerk and began his legal training.

The firm of Breeze, Jones & Casson had a busy practice, and the young clerk soon learnt the fundamental bread-and-butter details of rating, mortgages, insurance and drafting legal documents. He was soon a favourite with one of the partners, Randall Casson, and even joined the local Volunteers to which Casson belonged—the only military training Lloyd George ever had. About this time he also became involved with the local Liberal Association, as the senior partner, Breeze, was the Liberal agent for the area and used his young clerk for canvassing purposes.

As soon as he qualified, Lloyd George set up in his own solicitor's practice, firstly from the family home, which had now moved to Morvin House in Criccieth on the retirement of Uncle Lloyd from footwear manufacture, and later from his own offices at Portmadoc. He quickly began to win a reputation as an outspoken advocate who prepared his cases well. Defending quarrymen accused of net fishing on Nantlle lower lake, he attacked the bias of the magistrates against ordinary people who dared to fish. 'Tell me to whom you are referring?' demanded the chairman. 'I refer in particular to you, sir!' replied Lloyd George. The magistrates withdrew in high dudgeon, but when the court resumed, two of the quarrymen were acquitted and two received merely token fines. His outspokenness was always well calculated to produce the right effect. As a contributor to local papers on political matters his name was getting well known, and he was 'good copy' for local reporters who covered his activities with interest.

A pen portrait of the young solicitor at about this time was made by D. R. Daniel, later a friend and Liberal colleague, who met him outside Portmadoc police station in 1887:

> A young boyish man in simple clothes and Volunteer's leggings closed with laces on the legs. I remember his attractive smile and the incomparable brilliance of his lively blue eyes. He seemed nimble in mind and bearing, more daring in his views, more heroic in his look (though he smiled most of the time) than any of my other (political) friends.

The two instantly hit it off.

The following year a case came Lloyd George's way that made his name known throughout Wales. It arose out of the burial of an old quarryman in an Anglican churchyard extension in the tiny mountainside community of Llanfrothen, beside the reclaimed salt marshes which wind down towards Portmadoc alongside the River Glaslyn. The local vicar had been incensed that the quarryman's family wished to bury their relative beside his daughter (a dying wish) with the rites of his nonconformist denomination. He locked the churchyard gates against them, but Lloyd George had advised them to go ahead, as a new law of 1880 made burial of nonconformists in Anglican graveyards perfectly legal. The vicar sued the family and Lloyd George defended them in the County Court, where a jury found in their favour. However, after a delay of two months, the judge found in favour of the vicar. This incomprehensible decision was overturned on appeal to the High Court. It was seen as a test case and received wide publicity. It helped Lloyd George stand out in the Liberal Party, and he was made an alderman in the newly created Carnarvonshire County Council in 1889.

About this time he had started seeing Margaret Owen, the daughter of a tenant farmer who raised sheep and beef cattle on the hills above Criccieth. Lloyd George's reputation as a man attractive to women was already well established, and Miss Owen took some convincing that he might mend his ways under the stabilising influence of matrimony. Uncle Lloyd had been hoping that David would take an interest in a nice Baptist girl, instead of a Methodist as the Owens were, and the Owens also had their misgivings about Lloyd George, but love conquered all and they were married in the Methodist Chapel at Pencaenewydd, with Uncle Lloyd and a Methodist minister officiating. Within months an event occurred that was to change their lives and the lives of millions. This was the sudden death of the sitting Tory MP for Carnarvon Boroughs, Edmund Swetenham. The Lloyd Georges had planned a day out together when the fateful telegram arrived. Years later, Dame Margaret (as she became) described the scene:

> Presently my husband's train came in and I saw him looking as if he were anticipating a pleasant holiday. I had to tell him the news, and his smile vanished. We decided to go to Caernarvon but we had a miserable day! The shadow of the coming election spoilt everything!

Lloyd George had already been selected by the Liberal Association as their candidate for the now vacant seat and his Tory opponent was none other than the local squire, Ellis-Nanney of Gwynfryn Castle, on whose land Lloyd George's youthful poaching exploits had taken place! As usual, the Liberals worked hard on getting out and about to talk to the electorate, something by-elections make possible by freeing up many more volunteers and Party speakers than is the case at a general election when everyone is tied up in his own constituency. Thomas Gee, an influential Welsh nationalist, spoke for Lloyd George, who made some telling remarks for himself, and in this case it swung the marginal seat. On 10 April 1890, Lloyd George was elected by the slender margin of eighteen votes. 'The age of the cottage-bred man has at last dawned!' he declared. He was to hold the Carnarvon Boroughs seat with an increasing majority for the next fifty-five years, and, as several biographers have claimed, he would leave a greater mark on Britain than anyone since Oliver Cromwell.

The House of Commons that Lloyd George entered was dominated by the elder statesmen of the late Victorian era—Gladstone, the Grand Old Man of Liberal politics, and Lord Salisbury for the Conservatives. These men had lived through a period that was very different to that which Lloyd George and his future colleagues were to experience. Churchill would later write:

> Its small wars between great nations, its earnest disputes about superficial issues, the high, keen intellectualism of its personages, the sober, frugal, narrow limitations of their action, belong to a vanished period.

But to begin with, Lloyd George himself was concerned with narrow issues—mainly rural radical Welsh matters, like the conflict between tenant farmers and their landlords, the disestablishment of the Anglican Church in Wales (nonconformists had to pay tithes to an alien church), temperance, and Welsh nationhood. His early contributions to debates, delivered with a strong North Welsh accent, were dismissed as 'incoherent declamations'. It was some time before he learned to argue persuasively, and he admitted later, 'My first five years in Parliament were not a success.'

Meanwhile, the young MP and his growing family became established in London, although Margaret continued to regard Criccieth as her real home. A series of children—Richard, Mair, Olwen and Gwilym—were born between 1889 and 1894. The Lloyd Georges had a home in Criccieth, 'Bryn Awelon' (hill of breezes) overlooking the sea, and a flat in London. Lloyd George's brother William ran the Portmadoc office of Lloyd George & George solicitors, having qualified (with first class honours) after his brother, being articled at the same firm of Breeze, Jones & Casson. This provided a vital income, as MPs were not then paid a salary. Lloyd George helped by handling Welsh clients he picked up in London. He became keen on building up a Welsh national league within the Liberal Party organisation and connived at a Home Rule clause in the Welsh Disestablishment Bill, an attempt that severely damaged the ailing Liberal government. Accused of disloyalty by his future government colleague Asquith, it seemed to many that Lloyd George was mostly interested in personal and provincial power at the expense of his party.

He still had a nicely acerbic turn of phrase though, describing the Bishop of St Asaph's speech in defence of an established Welsh church as 'the Latinised tirades of an irate washerwoman'. He was a controversial backbencher and, in his own words, 'one of those harum scarum chaps who occasionally say and do wild things,'—an outsider, never at ease in upper class polite society, and much happier among self-made businessmen, journalists and fellow Welshmen. No layer of government or society overawed him, and he viewed senior civil servants, military chiefs, the aristocracy and even the royal family with a detached and critical eye. This helped him to assess each question on its practical merits alone. It has been claimed that he was always focused on the immediate problem—'the supreme pragmatic exponent of the short-run'—because as the economist Keynes said, 'In the long run we are all dead!'

He was a nonconformist in the broadest sense. Already with something of a reputation for louche morals with women, he was named in a paternity case by

Mrs Catherine Edwards, the wife of a Montgomeryshire doctor as the father of her child. William, acting on his brother's behalf, was able to refute the charge, but the additional pressure on his marriage did not help and Margaret spent increasing amounts of time at Criccieth. Lloyd George was left alone, living 'in cold draughty flats' and surrounded by all the temptations of a bachelor lifestyle in London.

There had also been an incident when he travelled to Argentina for the highly dubious Welsh Patagonian Gold Fields Syndicate in 1896. It was his first extended foray overseas and involved a long ocean voyage to South America. Many prominent Welsh businessmen had been persuaded by Lloyd George and others to invest in the company, and his trip was supposedly to check out the prospects. It turned out to be more of a pleasure cruise, with long days spent lounging on deck, reading novels, and later a pleasant trek through exotic countryside:

> The glens were lovely—clothed with palms, mimosa and cactus. Parrots—flights of them chattering around and an occasional humming bird [...] the scent of mimosa accompanied us everywhere. Each day we picnicked under the shade of a rock, or under the foliage of fine native trees—as a rule on the banks of bright little streams [...] after lunch we bathed in a pool. We had one moonlight ride which was most picturesque.

But even in Buenos Aires he was unable to keep his attentions from other people's wives. An Argentinian businessman sought satisfaction by challenging him to a duel and in order to avoid scandal at home, Lloyd George shaved off his trademark moustache and went into hiding at an obscure hotel until his ship sailed. It had still not regrown properly when he returned to the House of Commons, and the police failed to recognise him; when he appeared in the Chamber an opponent commented to his face that he had often wondered where Lloyd George's verbal asperity came from, but now he saw him without the moustache he quite understood!

With the private reverberations of the Edwards paternity case echoing in the background, Lloyd George busied himself with brisk parliamentary attacks on the Agricultural Land Rating Bill, which would have handed landowners a nice rate relief amounting from hundreds to thousands of pounds each while nothing was done for the poor. Lloyd George remarked:

> The contrast is too acute between the wealth and luxury of one class and the destitution and degradation of the other. One man works hard and has to recruit his exhausted strength in cramped quarters—another man who does nothing has allotted to him acres of breathing ground, walled up high so that he need not share its vitalising properties with those who have helped create his riches.

In another speech, he said:

It is not the soil but the soul which we want represented in the House of Commons. After all they [the Lords] have got a House all to themselves, which they guard as jealously as if it were a pheasant preserve!

Lloyd George and other radical MPs got themselves suspended by the Speaker so that the Bill would be delayed before the parliamentary recess. The correspondent of the *Daily Chronicle* commented:

He has a remarkable eye for weak points in debate and his keen criticisms have often been caught up later by the Front Opposition Bench and been adopted as the main line of attack [...] Of all the young men on the Liberal side Lloyd George has made the greatest mark of the session.

He was thanked by the Liberal leadership, and his friend, Herbert Lewis, describing Lloyd George's lifestyle at the time, said:

I was free to devote the whole of my time to Parliamentary work, but he made a great sacrifice. He was a poor man with a family of small children, living in a little flat and dependent on his profession for his daily bread [but] he threw himself heart and soul into Parliamentary work and I did my best to support him.

It is no longer fashionable to fight the class war in Parliament, but what should be realised is that it was thought even more impolite and impertinent in Lloyd George's day, when vast inequalities in living conditions needed to be challenged and overcome, than it is today, when few individuals have either the stomach or the wit to make an effective challenge against the privilege of, say, leading bankers, to mention but one class of protected beings! He was a demagogue, giving vent to the popular humours of the day, but that is how a politician who speaks for the ordinary people should be.

Lloyd George borrowed the rich imagery of his native Welsh nonconformist preachers and something of their emotional style. Speaking in a light tenor voice that carried well, he would declaim:

One man labours and yet starves, another lounges and still feasts [...] One set of men strive all the days of their lives in the vineyard, and yet amid the plenty and profusion which they themselves have helped to produce, sink unhonoured into a pauper's grave.

He gesticulated more freely than English members, and once described to a biographer how he reached out, literally, with his arm towards the people in the crowd. 'I reach out my hand to the people and draw them to me. Like children they seem then. Like little children.' A friend of the author's witnessed this as a small child when he saw Lloyd George, by then an old man, address a crowd at Manchester:

> He was wearing a dark cloak [his Tyrolean cape] and his long white hair and moustache were very striking and unusual. He seemed to reach out and sweep his arm over the audience as if drawing people to him, as if he was embracing us.

During 1896, he was also involved in supporting striking slate quarrymen against the autocratic feudal landowner and slate magnate Lord Penrhyn, whose castle near Bangor in North Wales was built entirely of slate. Some accused of rioting were defended in court by Lloyd George, who also helped raise strike funds. But his understanding of organised labour was mainly within a rural context. Later, his opposition effectively helped block the Education Bill of 1897, which would have provided funds for Anglican Church schools, and after the Jameson Raid fiasco in South Africa he criticised Joseph Chamberlain's jingoistic imperial policy at the Colonial Office as 'the pretensions of an electro-plated Rome, its peddling imperialism and its tin Caesar'—a swipe at Chamberlain's business in Birmingham where his family had made a fortune through defence contracts. A fellow Welshman, Ellis Griffiths, jocularly remarked, 'As the British Empire expands, the Chamberlain family contract.'

The first glimmerings of Lloyd George's future involvement with international conflict occurred during the Fashoda crisis of 1898. General Kitchener, his subsequent colleague in the Great War, had just fought one of the last little colonial wars against an inspired 'native' Dervish army that had been defeated at the Battle of Omdurman, near Khartoum in the Sudan, a disputed region claimed by Egypt, which was then really a British Protectorate and part of the Empire. Kitchener had encountered and confronted a much smaller French military mission at Fashoda on the Upper Nile under Capt. Marchand that had entered the region from the French Congo. Kitchener acted with great diplomacy in allowing British and French flags to fly side by side and travelled back to Europe with Marchand so that both might consult with their governments.

Most Conservatives and Liberals took a pro-imperialist stance, but Lloyd George went against the current:

> If we go to war and defeat France we shall be defeating the only power on the Continent with a democratic Constitution—[we shall be] the only countries where you have perfect civil and religious liberty in Europe, quarrelling with each other!

He was anticipating the Entente Cordiale between Britain and France by many years and basing it on democratic principle rather than merely strategic necessity. Did Lloyd George's lifelong Francophile tendencies influence his feelings of solidarity with France in 1914? We are bound to think that they did. Continental holidays were also helping to broaden his outlook at this time, with a cruise in the Mediterranean and trips to European resorts (while Margaret looked after the children at Criccieth) and an adventurous trip across Canada in the autumn of 1899.

The Canadian trip was officially to investigate the settlement possibilities for Welsh families. After sailing to Montreal, the party visited Ottawa and Toronto before heading west by steam train through seemingly endless forests. From the train, Lloyd George saw a native American and his squaw paddling a canoe along a forest river and in a small clearing filled with log cabins 'a number of children dancing and prancing out of a timber schoolroom, full of delight at their temporary emancipation', as he described it in a letter to his wife. He was stunned by the scale of the open prairies:

> There seems no end to it. Their method of locomotion here is mainly by buggies. Roads there are none—trails were the best we could hope for, mere tracks made by Indian wagons and perhaps parties such as ours.

They stayed in primitive timber lodges, sleeping on bug-infested straw pallets, and Lloyd George took the opportunity to spend several hours in the saddle, cantering alongside their buggy until he became very saddle sore and had to let his friend Llew Williams have a go on the 'bronco'.

In the Moose Mountains he saw lakes black with duck and the trees beginning to don their 'autumn garments of gold and precious stones', and in a clean hotel on a mountain lake they enjoyed fried eggs, wheat cakes, and jelly made from a little hardy cherry like sloe berries. At Banff, where their party had an official reception of uniformed Mounties, they stayed in the Hot Springs Hotel and Lloyd George was entranced by the scenery. 'It is Alpine in its magnificence ... though the foliage is much more variegated than in the Swiss valleys and the colours are therefore much finer.' Their visit to Vancouver on the west coast was brief, shortened by the worsening news from South Africa, the Welshmen making a faster return journey across Canada to be on board their ship at Montreal by the beginning of October. As they sailed for home, Lloyd George had already made up his mind to oppose the war against the Boer republics. 'The prospect oppresses me with a deep sense of horror. If I have the courage, I shall protest with all the vehemence at my command against the outrage which is perpetrated in the name of freedom.'

Though Lloyd George was a courageous orator with an interest in military history, he had no romantic illusions about war, which only the mass slaughter of 1914–18 eliminated from the minds of the late imperialist generation. He anticipated that the struggle would be long and costly, a setback to reform at home—'Every shell exploding in the African hills carries away an old age pension.' His sympathies were with the Boers, a small rural community, God fearing, a bit like the Welsh. They had tried to establish their own republic beyond the reach of British imperial power, but the discovery of gold and diamonds had led to the Jameson Raid. The British government used as a pretext the need for a system of democracy in the Boer republics. Demanding this of the conservative Boers and President Kruger was a screen for the commercial ambitions of men like Cecil Rhodes and British imperial expansion.

The Liberal Party in Parliament consisted of a pro-imperialist wing that supported the imperialist Conservative government in this policy (Cecil Rhodes was a subscriber to Liberal Party funds). Most of the other Liberals gave reluctant assent to the war, although the National Liberal Federation was largely anti-war and trade unions declared for a peace policy. Lloyd George's anti-war stance was almost unique and it made him the target of jingoistic hysteria. After a speech at Bangor he was struck on the head with a cudgel, his hat saving him from serious injury, and he was rescued by the police. He was burnt in effigy at Criccieth, along with effigies of his brother William and Uncle Lloyd! Cornish miners disrupted his speech at Liskeard. However, by far the most serious attack came at Birmingham, the home territory of Joseph Chamberlain MP, the Colonial Secretary and architect of the war whom Lloyd George had attacked for his connection to the firm of Kynoch, which had benefited from War Office contracts. Chamberlain had started out as a liberal radical, but then started to move to the right with the speed of light.

Lloyd George believed in the Empire; he just wanted it to consist of free states—home rule for everyone including Africa, Ireland, Wales and India, as well as Canada and Australasia. He hated the burning of farms and herding of women and children into camps where they died like flies. 'Military necessity cannot justify wrongdoing!' But he also believed that without Chamberlain's hard line insistence on complete capitulation by the Boer leaders during negotiations, Kitchener could have achieved a compromise peace.

The meeting at Birmingham Town Hall on 18 December 1901 was denounced by local daily papers, the *Birmingham Post* and the *Evening Mail*, as likely to end in riot. Crowds were waiting at New Street station when Lloyd George's train came in, but he was spirited away to a safe address. The Chief Constable warned him of the likely consequences of going ahead, and the chairman of the meeting, Alderman William Cook, cried off on doctor's orders. It is said that Lloyd George calmly smoked a cigar while he considered his options and decided not to disappoint his audience. As he arrived by carriage at the Town Hall, 350 police were holding back an ugly crowd of 30,000, many of whom were armed with sticks, knives and bricks wrapped in barbed wire. He managed to get inside, but when the doors were opened for ticket holders, everyone who could surged in, including many intent on violence. Pandemonium reigned inside the hall; as he tried to speak, the mob rushed forward and pelted those on the platform with missiles. Stones and bricks flew through the windows from outside and the glass dome of the hall started to cascade in. Lloyd George had to be smuggled into the basement where the wounded were being treated, eventually escaping disguised as a police constable.

The riot cost the lives of two people, including a policeman, and forty were hospitalised. When Lloyd George returned to Parliament, Chamberlain looked very angry. Years later, Lloyd George told Frances Stevenson that he heard him say, 'Someone has bungled badly', which is fairly ambiguous as to its meaning, but Lloyd George always believed that Chamberlain wanted him dead. He told another audience in Bristol soon after, 'It was necessary that we should hold this meeting at all hazards, to stand up for a great principle.' Lloyd George had moral courage and believed that reason must be made to prevail over sheer unthinking brute force.

Lloyd George was now listened to and respected on all sides of the House of Commons. His estimate of the length and outcome of the war had been more accurate than that of statesmen many years his senior who had been practising statecraft when he was still a boy at Llanystumdwy. His brilliant criticisms had been informed, illuminating and constructive, and lent him a new stature, not merely as a radical but also as a dominating parliamentarian.

In April 1902, his fifth child, Megan, was born. He had increased his majority in the recent elections at Carnarvon Boroughs. He was the most famous Welshman of the age, and now he stood on the threshold of a great career. Henry Campbell-Bannerman, the new Liberal leader, was expecting to form a Liberal government before long; Lloyd George, with the support of his wife and his country, was to be one of its rising stars.

# 2

# Icon of Empire

*He was like one of those revolving lighthouses which radiate momentary gleams of revealing light far out into the surrounding gloom, and then relapse into complete darkness.*
David Lloyd George on Kitchener

Kitchener's father, Henry Horatio Kitchener, was born in October 1805, the month of Nelson's famous victory and glorious death at Trafalgar. This laurel of martial glory was handed down to his son, who was named Horatio Herbert Kitchener in honour of the hero, but was always known by his middle name of Herbert.

Herbert Kitchener was the third child of the retired Indian Army colonel and his young wife, who after an unhealthy period of service in India had emigrated to Ireland to try their hand at estate improvement. Ballygoghlan, near the mouth of the River Shannon, consisted of a deserted village decimated by the potato famine of the 1840s and a ruinous estate house. Herbert was born at the nearby home of English family friends, the Sandes of Gunsborough Villa, in the summer of 1850. His father set about improving the farmland and the way his tenants operated, and soon found himself in conflict with the status quo. 'Improvement' necessarily led to increased rents, and some tenants whose families had farmed the land for generations could not afford these. Perhaps his experience in India led Colonel Kitchener to exercise a high-handed approach in dealings with the 'natives', but he suffered a severe reprimand from his neighbour, the Anglo-Irish aristocrat John Francis Eyre known as the Knight of Glin.

Colonel Kitchener, when evicting tenants who could not meet the increased rent, had ordered his bailiffs to set their dogs on the unfortunate family. Tradition dictated that they be horse-whipped before the roof was burned off their cottage, thus preventing their return. Incensed that families who had been faithful retainers of his own ancestors for generations should be treated in this manner, the Knight of Glin went down to an eviction and set his own dogs on the bailiffs, and when he met the colonel at Tralee races he openly challenged the 'upstart'. Not obtaining satisfaction, he gave him a sound horse-whipping in front of the large crowd.

This social setback did not deter the colonel from continuing his improvements, and by 1857 he had acquired another estate based on Crotta House, a seventeenth-century mansion that had once belonged to the famous Ponsonby family. As soon as they were old enough, Colonel Kitchener's children were put to work on the estates. Herbert became a competent horseman and was entrusted with herding cattle to market at Listowel and cutting turf. Once, while directing estate workers in cutting down trees, he struck a lad with his riding crop, doubtless copying the overbearing manner of his father, but the young man, James Sullivan, reacted with fury, pulling young Herbert from his horse and knocking him unconscious. To his credit, Herbert did not report the incident to his father.

Herbert had received only an elementary education at the village school in Ballylongford, and on hearing from the teacher that his son was a dullard, the colonel flew into a rage and threatened to apprentice the future field marshal to a hatter! The household was run like clockwork, strict discipline was enforced and even the maid serving breakfast had to wait outside the door before the clock in the hall struck the hour. The children were encouraged to develop stoicism, injuries were to be borne without complaint, and tale-telling was frowned upon. A governess and private tutors were hired, but a further report confirmed that Herbert had only a basic grasp of English and arithmetic as a teenager. However, his years in Ireland provided him with a very practical farming background plus an understanding of the lie of the land that served him well in the Army. Even as an elderly man on a visit to the old estates, after an absence of decades, he could recall the Irish field names.

Unfortunately for the colonel's successful farming ventures, his wife's health began to deteriorate in the mild but damp climate of south-west Ireland. Of a far more refined nature than her husband, Fanny Chevallier came from a family originating from Jersey and grew up in the gentrified environs of Aspall Hall in Suffolk. Her children and the colonel all adored her, but she was already a semi-invalid when it was decided to sell up and move to Switzerland for her health. Herbert was described at this time as a reserved, lanky youth, with piercing blue eyes and already with the trademark centre parting in his longish light brown hair. There is a curious story that his father had an aversion to sleeping under blankets, dating from his time in India, and used newspapers instead—possibly linked to some kind of skin affliction, which made him sweat profusely. Whether or not his wife's illness was linked to this practice is unclear, but whatever the case, her condition did not improve in the drier air of the Swiss mountains and she died in 1864.

Herbert and his brothers Walter and Arthur were sent to a school in Geneva for middle class English boys, where their Irish brogue was mocked by the pupils, who also made fun of their lack of educational ability. Herbert withdrew into himself after the death of his beloved mother and began to study in earnest, catching up in grammar, science, mathematics and beginning to learn French and German. Meanwhile, Colonel Kitchener had married Emma Green, his daughter Millie's music mistress, and bought an estate near Dunedin in New Zealand, which he visited with her in 1866. Another daughter, named Kawara, was born here the following year, but the Kitcheners soon returned to Europe, settling finally at Dinan in Brittany. In spring 1867, Herbert suffered a mental and physical breakdown and was sent to recuperate with his cousin Francis in Cambridge. He was prone throughout his life to a certain degree of temperamental instability which he controlled by withdrawing for short periods. Here he started a course of intense study, rounded off by a London 'crammer' who specialised in preparing young men for the entrance exams to Woolwich. Herbert had set his heart on becoming an officer in the Royal Engineers, despite his father's wish that he should try for the cavalry.

After passing the entrance exams for the Royal Military Academy at Woolwich, Herbert again found himself in an atmosphere of public schoolboys with their prejudices against cleverness and individuality. Fortunately, he as yet showed no sign of the former, but had to disguise the latter. Here he formed a friendship with an older cadet, Claude Conder, who introduced him to the study of Hebrew and an enthusiasm for bible studies. They both became keen exponents of Anglo-Catholicism, a more traditional form of Anglican worship that emphasised rituals of the Christian calendar. He found time for sport, writing to his sister Millie about a horse race he had taken part in with a wide water jump, 'a monstrous affair about 20 ft square and 5 ft deep, everybody went in. Some swam across, others stumbled through it. In fact it was a most amusing sight for all except those that were in the water like me.'

Later in the year he holidayed in Cornwall, staying at Truro, where he spent an enjoyable evening entertained by four young sisters who were also on holiday:

> Think of me with four young ladies, each longing for her swain. I really thought I should break a blood vessel or do something dangerous as they each caused great strain upon my legs. However [...] I enjoyed it very much as the candle which lighted us was put out quite by accident and we got on very well without it!

Although Herbert was never to marry, he clearly liked women and was attracted and attractive to them all his life.

Kitchener passed out from Woolwich at the end of 1870, 'below rather than above the standard of an R.E. Officer', and travelled to Brittany to spend Christmas with his father. Their relationship was now more easy-going and they discussed the exciting developments in the Franco-Prussian War then engaging Europe. Along with a fellow officer cadet, Kitchener decided to volunteer for the French ambulance corps to get some real experience. With the connivance of his father they were able to join Gen. Antoine Chanzy's Army of the Loire and helped ferry the wounded in field ambulances while a battle raged during January. However, Kitchener made the mistake of asking to be allowed to make an ascent in an observation balloon directing artillery fire. Unknown to him, his commission as a regular officer in the

British Army had been gazetted and he was now in strict breach of neutrality by this act. He also fell ill with pneumonia and pleurisy and was rescued from a wayside hovel by his father, who removed him to Dinan to recuperate.

After his recovery and the signing of an armistice by France and Germany, he returned to England where rumours of his adventure had reached the press. He was sent for by Field Marshal HRH the Duke of Cambridge, the commander-in-chief of the British Army, and given a severe dressing-down. Kitchener later remembered:

> He called me every name he could lay his tongue to, said I was a deserter and that I had disgraced the British Army. I never said a word. Then at the end, with a funny sort of twinkle, the Duke added, 'Well, anyhow boy, go away, and don't do it again!'

Kitchener could have lost his newly won commission and was strictly forbidden to speak of his adventure. Instead he was sent to the School of Military Engineering at Chatham, where he started to learn practical skills such as field fortification, surveying, mining and building construction. He was also introduced to the modern developments of telegraphy, photography and ballooning!

Because he enjoyed the more practical subjects, his instructors began to make favourable reports on him as a promising young officer and he was shortly appointed to become ADC to Brig.-Gen. George Greaves, who took him on a visit to witness manoeuvres by the Austro-Hungarian Army. In Vienna, Greaves fell ill and Kitchener took his place at all the inspections; he sat next to the Emperor Franz Josef, with whom he was able to converse in German. This was a great step up for a junior officer. On his return he was posted to a mounted troop of Royal Engineers at Aldershot Camp where he and his men practised techniques of field telegraphy during mock battles. He wrote to his sister:

> You know when I left Chatham I was posted to C troop RE. Since that I have been through Dartmoor manoeuvres where we were drenched with rain. Then hunting and work. Saturday last we had a good run and in the evening I dined with Prince Arthur. Was that not grand? Today I rode the Colonel's horse and had a capital day!

But Kitchener was getting bored with the routine, so when his friend Conder wrote to tell him that an officer was needed for his Palestine Exploration Fund survey he jumped at the opportunity. Conder, who was directing the survey as a lieutenant seconded to the Fund, asked for Kitchener, and the War Office sent him out in 1874 to join the expedition on the Plain of Philistia, once inhabited by the biblical Philistines. Here his enthusiasm breathed new life into the jaded survey party of Conder, three corporals and a clerk, who had already lost one member through endemic fever. One of the most satisfying periods of Kitchener's life now began, with plentiful opportunity for learning archaeological techniques, taking interesting photographs and studying Arabic as well as surveying. He also seemed to thrive in the warmer climate. The purpose of Army involvement in the survey was the production of the first detailed and accurate maps of the area and the gathering of military intelligence for future use. Ostensibly, the Palestine Exploration Fund were examining 'on-the-ground' evidence for bible stories and identifying the sites of events described.

Some scholars have found in this period of his life the key to the later man. 'His indomitable energy, his unequalled thoroughness, his hunger for work, his mastery of detail, his preparedness, his economy in men and material, his making sure of success, his preparedness for duty, his ability to inspire others with a zeal for work,' were thought by Prof. Daiches, a Palestine expert, to prefigure the great 'creator of armies' in 1915. Certainly, after his early lack of academic success, Kitchener demonstrated that he could assimilate a mass of detail in unfamiliar subjects and then produce a coherent and systematic result.

As his ship neared the Holy Land, he wrote:

> It was glorious, more from association than anything else, seeing for the first time that land which must be most interesting for any Christian. The sun rose in a golden halo behind the hills and we rushed towards it through the deep blue sea.

In addition to his technical skills he was soon to prove that he possessed the manly qualities of physical courage and presence of mind in an emergency. Conder was nearly swept out to sea in an undertow whilst swimming near Gaza, 'whence I was rescued by Lieutenant Kitchener'. Soon after, he was in trouble again when local tribesmen invaded their camp at Safed in Upper Galilee and Conder was involved in an altercation. 'They addressed me with many curses and the old man thrust his battle axe against my ribs.' As Conder was struck down by another man with a club, Kitchener rushed forward, using his Arabic to remonstrate with the attackers. Towering over them, he dominated the situation by his physical presence, allowing Conder to stagger away. The survey party retreated to a hill, followed by a shower of stones and the discharge of a musket. By sheer luck, a group of Turkish soldiers and the British Consular Agent arrived in the nick of time. Palestine was part of the Ottoman Empire at that time, and the British registered a strong protest with the authorities over the incident. The survey had to be suspended and both officers later gave evidence at the trial of the attackers, who received hefty fines.

Back in London, the friends collaborated on writing up their findings and producing an accurate map. Then, as Conder was unfit for field work, Kitchener took command of the survey. A colleague gave a vivid description of Kitchener at this time:

> We none of us thought much about our appearance and he least of all. After a few months in Palestine he looked more like a tramp than an officer in Her Majesty's Army. His clothes wouldn't have fetched a threepenny bit at an old clothes shop in Whitechapel!

But he was excellent company, full of life and high spirits. He wrote to his sister Millie, then living in New Zealand, 'Every day, from morning to night, I enjoy life amazingly.' Kitchener was also acquiring diplomatic skills, negotiating his party's progress with local officials and sheikhs, instead of just arriving unannounced, in order to avoid the former contentious results. Rising early, he and his companions would survey the hills and valleys, investigate the local wells and archaeological sites then take a midday siesta out of the fierce sun. In the cool of evening they would gather around the smoky camp fire to eat, serenaded by 'a babel of grunting camels and shouting servants'.

The Levant left a lasting impression on Kitchener. He produced a 'Guinea Book of Photographs of Biblical Sites' and took to wearing a full beard and sitting cross-legged on cushions dressed in Arab clothes, burning incense and drinking mint tea at his London flat. His brother Walter was amazed at the change in Herbert's personality. Far from the stiff, impeccably turned out field marshal of later years, young Kitchener anticipated the happy hippies by many decades. Few photographs of him remain from this period, but the Palestine Exploration Fund still treasure his original reports and letters. The secretary of the Fund at the time, Sir Walter Besant, wrote: 'Nothing has ever been done for the illustration and right understanding of the historical portions of the Old and New Testaments (since their translation) which may be compared with this great work.' The Fund also still has a number of early Palestinian artefacts acquired by Kitchener, some of which were declared skilful forgeries by a later expert. Was the young officer the unwitting dupe of a Middle Eastern 'antiques factory' or will some later expert declare them genuine after all? They certainly look convincing enough and modern technology is constantly reprising old canards.

In 1878, a war had begun between Russia and Turkey provoked by the 'Bulgarian atrocities' (a massacre of Christians by Turkish masters) and denounced forcefully in Britain by Gladstone, the Liberal statesman. Eager to see some action after the completion of his survey, Kitchener obtained letters of introduction to the Turkish authorities and travelled to Bulgaria. There he met Valentine Baker, a former British officer now serving as a major-general in the Turkish Army. Baker had been dismissed the British service after a conviction for attempted rape of a young woman in a railway carriage. He cut an impressive figure as a dashing officer, however, and the Turks had no qualms about employing him. His brother was the respected explorer Sir Samuel Baker. As we shall see, Kitchener later met and paid court to Valentine Baker's teenage daughter Hermione, one of the few women he entertained as a potential wife.

Kitchener was not impressed by the Bulgarians and was the victim of a con trick when a fellow traveller borrowed some money from him on the train with a promise to pay it back at journey's end but debunked at an intermediate station! He wrote an article about his trip for *Blackwood's Magazine*, but the real result of the Bulgarian interlude was the Treaty of Berlin, which settled the war by dividing up Turkey's possessions in the region. Two largely Muslim states, Bosnia and Herzegovina, were taken from Turkey and put under Austrian administration, thus sowing the seeds for the assassination that triggered the First World War. Britain was given ethnically divided Cyprus to govern, and Kitchener was selected by the Foreign Office to conduct a survey of the island.

Unfortunately, he did not get on too well with the island's new High Commissioner, Sir Garnet Wolseley, a celebrated soldier who had fought all around the world from Canada to Burma and liked to surround himself with officers he knew. He distrusted the taciturn but pushy Kitchener and was furious when his orders for the conduct of the survey were questioned behind his back by the junior officer who wrote to London for clarification of his position. Wolseley made this clear by taking charge of the funds for the survey, reducing its scale and being very parsimonious with money. One thing Kitchener did learn from him was always to stay on top of what was going on, but this inability to delegate to juniors and trying to do everything yourself has its drawbacks in a commander of vast enterprises. It worked for Wellington, in the Peninsular War, whose army never exceeded 100,000 men, and it worked for Wolseley commanding even smaller numbers in his colonial wars, but it almost led to disaster for Kitchener when he was ordering the fate of millions of men.

Kitchener had a brief sojourn as a military vice-consul in northern Turkey, which gave him a good insight into the workings of the Ottoman Empire, but he hated the cold winter. 'My house is all windows and consequently all draughts. It is impossible to warm it so you must excuse this writing as my hands are frozen,' he told his sister Millie. He praised his fur coat and the plentiful sables to be had, suggested she might like one and when returning to Cyprus, confessed, 'I was sorry to leave Anatolia with its lovely scenery and the glorious feeling of being the biggest swell in the country ... governors of districts here [Cyprus] do not back out of my presence!' It was during this period that some biographers believe Kitchener developed his large trademark moustache, having been impressed by versions he saw sported by fierce-looking Turkish officers.

Back in Cyprus under a new High Commissioner, he was able to conduct the survey on more ambitious lines, developing a land registry for the whole island. He also took part in horse racing and started the Cyprus Museum, becoming its first curator. In 1882, he wrote:

> Plenty of galloping over rocks. Office every day till 5 p.m. and then a ride if I can get one. I am doing some excavations amongst the old tombs at Salamis and have found a good lot of things. Only one gold ear ring in the precious metals but plenty of pots, pans, glass, alabaster and statuettes more or less broke.

He thought the British system infinitely superior in comparison with the former Turkish administration of Cyprus, with a just system of taxation based on land ownership and a network of district officers to administer the law impartially. He shared a house in Nicosia with another young officer, Lord John Kennedy of the Royal Scots Fusiliers, and they kept a bear cub as a pet which Kitchener had brought back from Anatolia. But just as the Cyprus survey neared completion, events in Egypt provided the catalyst for the next phase of Kitchener's life.

Thanks to an opportunistic move by Prime Minister Disraeli, Britain had recently acquired a major shareholding in the Suez Canal, along with the French, and when a nationalist Egyptian uprising occurred, military intervention to protect British interests and the 'gateway to India' was inevitable. By July 1882, a Royal Navy fleet was threatening Alexandria with bombardment when Kitchener took a week's 'sick leave' and hurried across from Cyprus. He contacted the fleet's military liaison officer and, with the help of Kitchener's fluent Arabic, the two officers went ashore in disguise to spy out the deployments of the nationalist army. After making notes and sketch maps, they were picked up by a launch from HMS *Inflexible*, the fleet's flagship, and taken on board to report. Kitchener stayed to watch the bombardment, but the High Commissioner in Cyprus was demanding his return to duty. Before he went, he made contact with the ADC of Sir Henry Evelyn Wood, who was to be appointed the Sirdar (commander) of the Egyptian Army after the defeat of the nationalists. The contact paid off when in December he was offered a two-year engagement as second-in-command of an Egyptian cavalry regiment and he bade farewell to Cyprus for good.

As second-in-command to Lt Col. Taylor, Kitchener became responsible for selecting men and training Egyptian cavalry units. He was promoted first to captain in the British Army and then became a major in the Egyptian Army in a matter of days. That he was an excellent horseman and a daring intelligence operative had clearly helped in obtaining this preferment for a mere 'sapper', as Royal Engineers officers were known.

John Macdonald, a correspondent for the *Daily News*, described 'a tall, slim, thin-faced figure in long boots, "cut-away" dark morning coat and an Egyptian fez tilted over his eyes'. Early one morning, Macdonald, Kitchener and Taylor drove in the raw, greyish January to meet the Fellaheen (peasant) cavaliers. Taylor did most of the talking, Kitchener expressing himself with the occasional nod or monosyllable. 'He's quiet,' Taylor whispered. 'That's his way,' and with a jerk of the head, 'he's clever!' Taylor had obviously been told of his second-in-command's resourcefulness and was consequently prepared to overlook his apparent reticence.

Kitchener stood in the middle of the riding circle, looking like a circus master, while the Egyptians mounted and rode around him. Their performance was poor, but the least unfit were chosen to become native officers. 'We'll have to drive it into these fellows,' grunted Kitchener, thinking aloud. Later he wrote, 'The same blood courses in their veins as those wild Arabs of the desert. Discipline, discipline, discipline—that is the one thing needful.'

The light blue uniforms chosen for the cavalry drew some scorn from other regiments when they first appeared on parade, Kitchener receiving unfair criticism and ridicule for this. Having never been one for club gossip, he avoided officers' clubs and socialised instead with the officers he knew and with locals, including the Egyptian Prime Minister, Nubar Pasha, from whom he learned something of Egyptian diplomacy. During 1883, he was also initiated into the Freemasons in Cairo and remained an active mason throughout his career. It is quite likely that his membership of this secret brotherhood assisted his preferment, as many highly influential senior figures were members of the organisation. He was also seeing Hermione Baker, the 16-year-old daughter of Gen. Valentine Baker. The previously disgraced general was now head of the Egyptian gendarmerie, a paramilitary police force, and the Bakers lived in Cairo.

Late in the year, Kitchener spent his leave in the Arabah Valley near the Gulf of Aqaba, helping to conduct a survey for the Palestine Exploration Fund investigating the sites of the biblical desert of Exodus. During the two months' leave he came to detest his academic colleague, Prof. Edward Hull, a timid geologist, and the two parted after reports were received of fighting in the Sudan. Hull returned a slower, safer way via Gaza, while Kitchener set out on camels with four Arab guides across the 200-mile wide and virtually waterless Sinai Desert. He wrote:

> We passed a good many Arabs of the tribes and I was received among them as Abdullah Bey, an Egyptian official, thus reviving a name well known and revered amongst them: they supposed me a relation of the great Sheikh Abdullah. I was everywhere well received. But the last two days' travelling were among the most trying I have ever experienced; a very strong west wind blew the sand right up into our faces, so that the camels could hardly face it. I travelled every day from 8 a.m. to 6 p.m. and with very little variation. One night we had to travel a good deal after dark to make a brackish pool of water and I very nearly lost the party as we had to separate to hunt for the water.

In the days before helicopters and all-terrain vehicles, Kitchener travelled as Lawrence of Arabia and many other adventurous Britons did—like a native.

The damage to his eyes and face caused by the glare and blown fragments of sand and scrub was to leave a lasting impression on his features. His eyes henceforth wore a bleak and wind-battered look, with the left one slightly out of synch, and his skin, later described by Winston Churchill as bloated and purplish, was thought by Lord Esher to be 'as coarse as a common soldier's.' Towards the end of Kitchener's life, the writer J. B. Priestley said that the old soldier's eyes looked somehow 'jellied', which added to his monolithic quality as 'a great idol rather than a man'.

Whatever the damage to his features, Kitchener was welcomed back in Cairo with enhanced stature and some admiration for his enterprise, even from those who disliked his personality. The defeat of General Hicks' punitive expedition in the Sudan had led to a need for intelligence officers in the region to find out what was going on, and Kitchener was one of the officers sent to Berber. He was to maintain contact across the desert with General Gordon, who had been made Governor of Khartoum but was virtually cut off by a fanatical army of Ansar (helpers), followers of the charismatic Mahdi (the chosen one), who despite his religious enthusiasm had made an unholy alliance with Osman Digna, a well-established Arab slave trader controlling the Red Sea coastline.

British policy was similar to that of the Americans in Afghanistan in recent times. Local tribes were sounded out and their allegiance or neutrality was bought with gold and silver. Some supplied Kitchener with a personal bodyguard of up to twenty Arab tribesmen, with whom he swore oaths of blood brotherhood. Wearing Arab clothes, they galloped together over the desert wastes. The solitude of the desert, the need for personal survival, and something of the fatalism of the tribes subtly altered Kitchener's perspectives. At night it was bitterly cold and by day they were scorched by the sun. Biting insects and snakes were the only living creatures apart from themselves, and life was cheap, but never before or after did he feel so good. In those days he 'tasted of the salt of the earth'.

'Just got back from 17 days desert ride and rather exciting hunt of one of the Mahdi's emirs,' he wrote to Sir Walter Besant at the PEF. It was during these covert operations that he witnessed a spy being flogged to death at Dongola by the Mudir, the local ruler who was playing a shifty game with the British. 'Death at their hands I did not fear,' Kitchener told a friend, 'in fact I expected it. But such a death!' From this time he carried a bottle of cyanide as his insurance in case he was captured. The harsh desert made Bedouin tribesmen look upon kindness as weakness, and gratitude as stupidity. They were cruelly indifferent to suffering.

Kitchener was able to smuggle messages to and from Gordon in Khartoum, and eventually Gladstone's Liberal government back home reluctantly authorised a relief expedition, commanded by Sir Garnet Wolseley, to set out into the desert. The British press went wild with enthusiasm and Kitchener's name, as the main link with Gordon at great personal risk, was on everyone's lips. All were hopeful. Gordon noted in his journal:

> Major Kitchener, the man I have always placed my hopes upon [...] one of the very few superior British officers with a hard constitution, combined with untiring energy [...] Whoever comes up here had better appoint Major Kitchener Governor-General, for it is certain, after what has passed, I am impossible, (what a comfort). 15 December 1884: Now mark this, if the expeditionary force does not come in ten days, the town may fall; and I have done my best for the honour of my country. Goodbye. C. G. Gordon.

On 26 January 1885, Gordon was still holding out, even though Ansar spies had infiltrated his native garrison troops. The Mahdi attacked, realising he had just days before the arrival of the relief force, and the city fell amid scenes of appalling cruelty. Gordon was speared in the Palace gardens and his head cut off. When it was presented to the Mahdi, the enraged leader cried, 'Why do you not obey me!' He had given instructions for Gordon to be taken alive.

The anticlimax of this calamity shattered the pride of late Victorian Britain. The relief force was ordered to retire, and the Sudan was abandoned to the enemy. Kitchener was asked to write an official report on the fall of Khartoum for Wolseley. He wrote:

> The memorable siege of Khartoum lasted 17 days [...] due to the indomitable resolution and resource of one Englishman. Never was a garrison so nearly rescued, never was a commander so sincerely lamented.

A further personal tragedy awaited Kitchener in Cairo. His intended fiancée Hermione Baker had died of typhoid fever, aged just 18, at about the same time that Gordon was murdered in Khartoum. For many years afterwards, Kitchener wore a locket containing her hair next to his skin.

Kitchener was then occupied with Wolseley in rooting out native chiefs and even highly placed Egyptians who had secretly colluded with the Mahdists or intrigued against the British. On one occasion during an interrogation he was recognised by a prisoner and attacked, almost being throttled to death before guards could prise off his athletic attacker. In June he was gazetted a lieutenant colonel as a reward for his services, but he soon after resigned his commission in the Egyptian Army and sailed for home, telling his sister Millie, 'I am such a solitary bird that I often think I were happier alone.'

Other passengers looked with awe on the tall and lonely figure studying books on Arabic, with his dark sunburnt features, intimidating moustache and air of reserve. Meanwhile, out across the whistling desert sands, another fate was overtaking the conqueror of the Sudan. Death took the Mahdi in the height of his glory, some say by the poison-wielding hand of a jealous concubine. But whatever the reason, Kitchener sailed grimly home.

In London he found himself a celebrity, being presented to Queen Victoria with other Sudan expedition officers. He was a 'must have' on every country house guest list. His new friend, the socialite and former Liberal MP Pandeli Ralli, invited the now famous soldier to regard his house in Belgrave Square as his own. The two men shared an interest in Levantine civilisation and all things French, and Ralli also gave invaluable advice on which invitations to accept from society hostesses.

Soon Kitchener was back in Africa—first as a Boundary Commissioner in Zanzibar, and when on his way to Cairo he was appointed Governor-General at Suakin on the Red Sea coast. Here his old adversary Osman Digna was still a local source of trouble, and after fortifying the town, Kitchener headed out with a force of mixed regular and irregular native troops stiffened by British officers to try and seize the troublesome Dervish leader. (The British described all Mahdists as 'Dervishes', although strictly these were members of a mystical Islamic sect.)

The fact that he had been positively ordered not to attempt a military expedition did not dissuade him. Osman Digna was only fifteen miles away, and the early morning attack seemed to go well at first. The Sudanese infantry, mainly blacks who hated the slave-trading Arabs, overran the Dervish village, but the native cavalry following met ferocious fire from the enemy and faltered. It was while he was trying to rally the men that Kitchener's aides saw him lurch in the saddle. A bullet had struck him in the angle of his jaw, splintering the bone and penetrating his neck. He was evacuated and the force retreated, leaving 200 dead Dervishes, Osman Digna wounded but still free, and about forty casualties among the attackers.

Kitchener was taken by steamer to hospital in Cairo where his wound was regarded as serious as it had become infected. 'A splinter of bone has embedded itself close to his windpipe and tonsils,' an aide wrote to Millie. 'He cannot yet talk.' Queen Victoria telegraphed for news and the British press hailed the action as a victory for imperial arms against a savage foe. The wound seems not to have disfigured his face, but he told friends that the bullet had eventually made its way into his throat and that 'with a desperate effort' he swallowed it and nature did the rest! In those days, bullets from Dervish muskets were usually round and made of lead.

He seems to have tapped into a popular taste for action in the Sudan. When his condition was improving, the Sirdar, Sir Francis Grenfell, visited and told him he ought to be court-martialled for disobeying orders but that he had become a hero instead! On a recuperative visit home, Kitchener met Lord Salisbury, the new Tory Prime Minister, and was again invited to meet Queen Victoria, before being sent back as second-in-command to the Sirdar. A new expedition was mounted and this time with British troops in the fighting line, a force of 6,000 Dervishes was defeated at a cost of 200 casualties to the Egyptian Army. Kitchener successfully and skilfully led the entire Egyptian cavalry to reconnoitre the area and then drew the enemy into a carefully laid ambush of infantry and artillery.

What kind of man had Kitchener become? He was generally unpopular among the officers of the Army as a reserved and aloof man who was uninterested in the usual club activities of Cairo. He was also disliked for being promoted over the heads of more experienced officers who had led humdrum lives obeying orders and doing what was expected of them. Hard riding in the desert had made his lean frame tough and muscular, and he was dedicated to a cause—the recovery of the Sudan and avenging Gordon, for whose death he felt a personal responsibility. To do this he would go to any lengths. After his sweetheart Hermione died, his heart was hardened and romantic love had died with her. Henceforth, his women friends were all of the more mature type and usually married. He now lived for his work alone. And his work was nothing less than the promotion of Britain's imperial destiny.

# 3

# The Lion Cub

*It was the nation that had the lion heart ... I had the luck to be called upon to give the roar.*
Winston Spencer Churchill

At the birth of Churchill one feels some remarkable natural event might have taken place to signal the momentous occasion. But, no, the future 'greatest Briton' first saw the light of day in a small, bleak bedroom deep in the heart of Blenheim Palace in Oxfordshire. He was there only because his mother had gone into premature labour as a result of 'a rough drive in a pony carriage', and so Britain's foremost statesman of the twentieth century arrived in a hurry on 30 November 1874, a whole two months before he was officially expected. There were no rumblings of celestial thunder, the goats did not 'run affrighted from the hills', as Shakespeare claims marked the birth of the great patriot Glyndwr; not even a comet was in sight.

Churchill was certainly not 'in the common run of men', but was always the first to poke fun at himself, and did so with great eloquence in his book *My Early Life*, which later inspired the film *Young Winston*. His father was Lord Randolph Churchill, newly married to the American socialite Jennie Jerome, whose glittering, lithe, panther-like profile was celebrated throughout fashionable society. Winston's earliest memories were of Ireland, where Lord Randolph had accompanied his father, the Duke of Marlborough, as his secretary, when that august personage had been appointed Lord Lieutenant of the sister isle. His earliest memory was the unveiling of a statue by his 'formidable Grandpa' and of the old man's loud speech to the 'great black crowd, with scarlet soldiers on horseback'. The next occasion was, however, to be less pleasant:

My nurse, Mrs Everest, was nervous about the Fenians. I gathered these were wicked people and there was no end to what they would do if they had their way [...] on one occasion, when I was out riding my donkey, we thought we saw a long dark procession of Fenians approaching. We were all much alarmed, particularly the donkey, who expressed his anxiety by kicking; I was thrown off and had concussion of the brain. This was my first introduction to Irish politics!

Churchill remembered his mother as being someone who 'shone for me like the evening star—I loved her dearly, but at a distance. My nurse was my confidant. Mrs Everest it was who looked after me and tended all my wants.' The life in Ireland suited Lord Randolph and his bride. They spent much time hunting:

> My picture of her in Ireland is in a riding habit, fitting like a skin and often beautifully spotted with mud. She and my father hunted continually on their large horses; and sometimes there were great scares because one or the other did not come back for many hours after they were expected.

Jennie's family were of Huguenot extraction and had emigrated to America in the 1700s. Her father, a successful newspaper tycoon, had been American Consul at Trieste, and for three years Jennie lived with her mother and sisters at the court of Napoleon III in Paris, where she learned several languages and court etiquette in the European capital of manners until the Franco-Prussian war drove them to settle in London. Jennie met Lord Randolph at a Cowes Regatta and they were engaged three days later. The Churchills were nothing if not precipitate!

Winston's first attempts at mastery of the English language began even before the appearance of the governess who was to give him the rudiments of education. 'Mrs Everest produced a book *Reading Without Tears*. It certainly did not justify its title in my case.' Before the dreaded governess arrived, he hid in the extensive shrubberies surrounding the Viceregal Lodge in Dublin, thus revealing an early propensity for eluding would-be pursuers. Winston was not a good pupil, although he had an excellent retentive memory and a great talent for any subject that interested him. The problem was that few subjects given prominence in those days—ancient Latin and Greek, mathematics and organised games—actually did appeal to the unorthodox 'troublesome boy' he became. Sadly, his earliest years of formal education at an expensive preparatory school were very unhappy. The young pupils, including Winston, were savagely beaten with the birch for all manner of trivial mistakes, until after two years of continual anxiety his health broke down and he was removed. His next school before Harrow was run by two kindly old ladies in Brighton, and here he spent a happy time recovering his health and learning subjects like French, history, poetry, riding and swimming, which he thoroughly enjoyed.

It was during holidays from the harsh preparatory school that Winston first found solace and an outlet for his pent-up frustration by ranging his toy soldiers across the nursery floor and fighting mock battles with them, just as his illustrious ancestor, John Churchill, the first Duke of Marlborough, had fought real battles and gained immortal fame as England's outstanding general of all time. Winston's favourite reading then was Robert Louis Stevenson's *Treasure Island*, which provided him with an escape from uncongenial reality to a world of buccaneering adventure and derring-do.

The time came for him to sit the Harrow School entrance examination; unfortunately, it was in Latin:

> I wrote my name at the top of the page. I wrote down the number of the question '1'. After much reflection I put a bracket round it thus '(1)'. But thereafter I could not think of anything connected with it that was either relevant or true. Incidentally there arrived from nowhere in particular a blot and several smudges. I gazed for two whole hours at this sad spectacle.

Fortunately, the headmaster Mr Welldon decided 'from these slender indications of scholarship' that Winston was worthy to pass into Harrow. Because of his absence of skill in ancient languages he was kept in the Lower Form for about three years, during which time he was intensively instructed in the use of English by an excellent tutor, Mr Somervell, who taught a system of English analysis that enabled him to attain mastery of 'the ordinary British sentence—it is a noble thing'. This was to be put to good use later.

Winston regarded his schooldays as a grey patch in his life, although there were various highlights. He won a prize for reciting Macaulay by heart, and the public schools' fencing championship. His views were expressed in this interesting passage:

> I would far rather have been apprenticed as a bricklayer's mate, or run errands as a messenger boy, or helped my father to dress the front windows of a grocer's shop. It would have been real; it would have been natural; it would have taught me more; and I should have done it better. Also I should have got to know my father, which would have been a joy to me.

He then presents a philosophical musing:

> The prolonged education indispensable to the progress of Society is not natural to mankind. It cuts against the grain. A boy would like to follow his father in pursuit of food or prey. He would like to be doing serviceable things so far as his utmost strength allowed [...] He would ask little more than the right to work or starve.

Alas, Winston did not know his father well, and his dreams of following him into Parliament as his valuable right-hand man were never to be realised. Lord Randolph was the parliamentary leader of the so-called Tory democracy group, who appealed over the heads of the aspiring Liberal middle classes directly to some supposed common interest between the ordinary working man and the Tory squirearchy. This was in the days before the extension of the vote to all classes, when the Labour Party was the dream of a small group of disregarded socialists. (It did not exist until 1900.) Lord Randolph achieved his appeal by being memorably rude in a witty way to all who either opposed or offended him. He made good newspaper copy, and his every speech was reported verbatim. His striking appearance, goggle eyes, dandyish outfits and large moustache drew admiring glances from working men everywhere, who felt he was fighting their corner with the 'toffs'.

It worked to a certain extent, as he was made Secretary of State at the India Office, presided over the annexation of Burma, and became Chancellor of the Exchequer and Leader of the House in Lord Salisbury's Tory government. But, like his son, he was a pioneering maverick who thought he might hustle the Cabinet into doing things his way. A misjudged resignation resulted in the end of his governmental career, and an illness, possibly syphilis or a brain tumour, clouded his declining years until his death at the early age of 45. Apart from his name, the only useful legacy he bequeathed to his son was an early initiation into the Freemasons.

Lord Randolph was not a good father. Winston recalled only two occasions when he got especial attention—once when on reviewing his son's 1,500 toy soldiers drawn up in battle array he asked if Winston would like to join the army, and once when he told him off for firing a shotgun near the library windows:

> For years I thought that my father with his experience and flair had discerned in me the qualities of military genius. But I was told later that he had only come to the conclusion that I was not clever enough to go to the Bar.

Denied a glittering career as a barrister, Winston seemed destined as 'food for powder', the fate another selfish and undiscerning parent, the Countess of Mornington, had a hundred years before earmarked for a supposedly dull son— eventually the Duke of Wellington and conqueror of Napoleon! But it suited his tastes ideally. Within weeks of going to Harrow he had joined the Rifle Corps and spent several years in the school's Army Class, which let him off many subjects like Latin and Greek that he would rather have avoided anyway.

An accident caused by a jump from a bridge whilst eluding pursuers, including his younger brother Jack, during a holiday game, delayed his attempts to get into the Military College at Sandhurst but gave him time during recuperation to observe his father's performances in the House of Commons from the distinguished Strangers' Gallery and to witness Mr Gladstone's speech on the Home Rule Bill (for Ireland).

> The Grand Old Man looked like a great white eagle, at once fierce and splendid. His sentences rolled forth majestically and everyone hung upon his lips and gestures, eager to cheer or deride. [...] But Mr Gladstone, shaking his right hand with fingers spread claw-like, quelled the tumult and resumed [his speech].

Thanks to the efforts of an Army crammer, Winston scraped into Sandhurst on his third attempt at the entrance exam in 1893, but did so well on the year-long course that he passed out eighth in his batch of 150 cadets. Because he wanted to join the cavalry (he was mad about horses and thought the uniforms better) his father wrote him a very disparaging letter on his lack of attainment, mainly it seems because of the extra costs entailed by the equestrian needs of a cavalry subaltern, which in India would include a string of polo ponies. In mitigation, however, Lord Randolph was by this time desperately ill. A world cruise had failed to restore his health and he returned to London, dying in January 1895, just a month before his son was commissioned as a second lieutenant in the 4th Hussars. Now technically head of the family, Lady Randolph held the purse strings, and Winston's extravagance was a continuing source of friction—he always took the view that expenditure should be ruled by needs not resources. However, she was always willing to pull strings for him to further his career, and their collaboration henceforth was 'more like brother and sister than mother and son.'

One such string pulling resulted in his first taste of military action, in Cuba of all places. Here the Spanish Army was attempting to put down an insurgency and, with the necessary permissions, Churchill and another subaltern took passage for New York *en route* for Havana. He was lavishly entertained in New York by one of his mother's admirers, Bourke Cockran, an American politician of whom Churchill was later to say, 'He was my role model.' In Cuba, whilst marching with a column of troops through the forest, Churchill first came under fire. A horse just behind him in file was struck by a bullet:

> There was a circle of dark red on his bright chestnut coat. He hung his head but did not fall. Evidently he was going to die, however, for his saddle and bridle were soon taken off him [...] I began to take a more thoughtful view of our enterprise than I had hitherto done.

The following night they again came under fire as they lay in hammocks slung in a barn. Bullets ripped through the flimsy thatch.

> The Spanish officer whose hammock was slung between me and the enemy's fire was a man of substantial physique. I have never been prejudiced against fat men. At any rate I did not grudge this one his meals. Gradually I dropped asleep.

Churchill arrived with his regiment at Bombay in the autumn of 1896, when the British Empire and the Indian Raj was at its height. In his eagerness to get ashore, he dislocated his right shoulder grabbing at a mooring ring while stepping from a pitching launch, an accident that may have saved his life—he preferred to use an automatic pistol instead of his sword during close-quarter fighting ever afterwards. But it hampered his growing interest in the game of polo, which he had to play with his shoulder strapped up. On the third night, he and brother officers were invited to dine with the Governor of the Bombay Presidency, Lord Sandhurst, who made the mistake of kindly asking the young officer's opinion on some question.

Churchill later recalled, 'I have forgotten the particular points of British and Indian affairs upon which he sought my counsel; all I can remember is that I responded generously.' After a splendid evening, the young soldiers had to be assisted back to their encampment.

At Bangalore, above 3,000 feet in the cooler climate which suited a profusion of European roses, Churchill's cavalry cantonments proved delightful. Here a well-regulated life on the parade grounds and the shady tree-lined avenues between the spacious bungalows was lived by British officers who cantered about their business on a string of horses. Churchill's bungalow had a paddock of about two acres and a barn containing the chargers, polo ponies and runabout hacks he and two brother officers shared. 'Just before dawn every morning one was awakened by a dusky figure with a clammy hand adroitly lifting one's chin and applying a gleaming razor to a lathered and defenceless throat.' This was one of three Indian butlers who catered for all the officers' domestic needs. After cavalry drill and breakfast in the Mess, stables inspection was followed by luncheon in the Mess, and then it was back to the bungalow for a midday siesta out of the blistering heat. In the cool of evening, chukka after chukka of polo was played, followed by hot baths, dinner to the strain of the regimental band and the clinking of ice in well-filled glasses. 'Such was the long, long Indian day as I knew it for three years; and not such a bad day either.'

But Churchill was convinced that to get on he needed more experience. He believed, erroneously as it turned out, that his life would be a short one like his father's had been. First, he started ordering books to complete his education—history, philosophy, politics—anything his mother could send out to him. Secondly, he tried to get in on every active service opportunity, and his first chance arose when joining the punitive expedition of Sir Bindon Blood against the Pathan tribes of the North West Frontier. Sir Bindon was a family friend and a proud descendant of the notorious Col. Thomas Blood, who in the reign of Charles II had attempted to steal the Crown Jewels from the Tower of London, for which act, after having been pardoned, he was made Captain of the King's bodyguard! With General Blood's connivance in the Mamund Valley, Churchill had his first taste of action, returning fire against Pathans hidden in the rocks, when he witnessed the adjutant falling wounded and being slashed by a swordsman as he lay helpless. 'I forgot everything else at this moment except a desire to kill this man.' Churchill advanced, brandishing his cavalry sword; then as he saw more tribesmen approaching, he drew his revolver and took aim. He fired several shots with none taking effect, other than to drive the sword wielder behind a rock.

The upshot of all this, apart from newspaper articles sent back to Britain by the budding war correspondent, was an 85,000-word book, *The Story of the Malakand Field Force*, which if not a literary sensation was still widely read, despite being 'corrected' for publication by a mad Anglo-Irish uncle with eccentric notions of punctuation. Churchill even received an admiring letter from the Prince of Wales, later Edward VII. The success of his first book encouraged the author and he launched on an even more profitable enterprise, his one and only novel, entitled *Savrola*, the story of a young hero and an older patrician woman. In later life he said, 'I have consistently recommended my friends not to read it!'

Churchill next tried very hard to get on the Tirah expedition under Gen. Sir William Lockhart, a hero of the Indian Mutiny who had been fighting on the frontiers for forty years. Although he managed to get himself attached to the general's staff, the threat of action fizzled out, but with his journalistic curiosity and historian's instinct he still gained much useful knowledge from the old general and helped him with some political and press relations advice. Meanwhile, a far more important campaign had opened in the Sudan, and Churchill determined to be part of it.

# 4

# Challenge to Empire

Gen. Sir Herbert Kitchener, Sirdar of the Egyptian Army, was dancing the wild fandango in his pyjamas in the middle of the night, with a lamp in one hand and a telegram from London in the other. It had just been decoded by two delighted junior officers who brought it straight across to his residency and roused the reluctant Sirdar. He let them in himself, after much persuasion, and read 'You will advance into the Sudan'—the words he had been waiting to hear ever since he became commander-in-chief four years before.

Kitchener's appointment as Sirdar had much to do with the recommendations of one man, Lord Cromer, the British Agent in Egypt, who controlled the Egyptian government's purse strings. The two men understood one another. Kitchener was not to engage in any wild and unnecessary expenditure, despite his Egyptian troops being so badly dressed in worn-out uniforms that they looked like a band of paupers. The young Egyptian Khedive (Viceroy) was so incensed by this that he denounced Kitchener in front of the troops, but had to apologise after Kitchener threatened resignation. With the problem of the Dervishes looming, this was not a good idea.

The first move was an advance across the desert to Atbara, where British and Egyptian troops defeated 20,000 Dervishes after a full-frontal attack on their fortified stronghold, resulting in 568 casualties to Kitchener's army, about 3,000 Dervish dead and 2,000 prisoners. Kitchener's old adversary Osman Digna and his piratical followers escaped, but the Dervish leader Mahmoud was captured and paraded in chains. The next step was to construct a railway across waterless desert to bring up supplies and more troops. Royal Engineer officers found two wells in the 200 miles of trackless waste by water divining, enabling the project to go ahead. At this point, Lord Cromer in Cairo panicked as he was expected to find funds for the whole campaign, without help from London. Kitchener again threatened to resign until the two men had a conference and matters were ironed out, with the funds for work on the Aswan Dam being used up instead!

In August 1898, with 400 miles of military railway now available to transport supplies and men, Kitchener began his final advance on Khartoum. He had about 25,000 men—half the estimated strength of the Dervishes remaining under the Khalifa, the Mahdi's successor. There were about 8,000 British troops, including one battalion of the 21st Lancers who were to act as scouts and a cavalry screen, supplied by a reluctant War Office in London that very much resented Kitchener's high-handed demands and his lording it over their troops when he was merely an Egyptian officer.

Arriving at the last minute, 2$^{nd}$ Lt Winston Churchill had reported to the cavalry barracks in Cairo after a hard-fought campaign to be included. All his requests had been turned down by Kitchener, even including a telegram from the Prime Minister Lord Salisbury, who had been impressed by Churchill's book *The Story of the Malakand Field Force* and had written requesting that the young man be allowed to join the 21st Lancers. Finally, Sir Henry Evelyn Wood, in charge at the War Office, overruled the Sirdar as Churchill was to be attached to a British Army unit, and he was rushed out just in time.

Kitchener's force also included ten gunboats and transport steamers towing Egyptian sailing boats loaded to the gunwales, which shadowed the Army by advancing up the Nile. The plans for the entire campaign were in his head. 'If anything had happened to him everything would have ground to a halt,' a staff officer said. His operations room was chaotic, with papers and plans showing dispositions and manoeuvres with little flags strewn all over the floor. Nothing was properly filed or indexed, his staff officers were used as runners to brigade commanders and rarely asked or offered opinions, and his divisional commanders were ordered about like schoolboys. All his Egyptian Army officers were hand picked and loyal to 'the chief', but the British Army officers resented him. They realised, however, that he knew more about fighting in the desert than any of them.

Churchill described his journey 1,400 miles into the heart of North Africa:

We were transported by train then stern-wheeled steamers to Aswan, led our horses around the cataract at Philae, re-embarked and voyaged for four days to Wadi Halfa, then proceeded 400 miles by the marvellous military railway whose completion had sealed the fate of the Dervish power.

At each staging post he was haunted by the fear that he might be sent back on the Sirdar's orders. 'However, as the stages of the journey succeeded one another, hope began to grow in my breast.' Arrived at the Atbara camp, with 200 miles of desert to march across towards Khartoum and the coming battle, Churchill was finally confident that he had slipped through the net. He wrote:

Nothing like the battle of Omdurman will ever be seen again. Everything was visible to the naked eye. The armies marched on the crisp surface of the desert plain through which the Nile wandered in broad reaches, now steel, now brass. Cavalry galloped in close order and infantry, or spearmen, stood upright ranged in lines or masses to resist them […] Batteries of artillery or long columns emerged from the filmy world of uneven crystal [mirage] onto the hard yellow ochre sand and took up their positions among jagged red-black rocks with violet shadows. Over all the immense dome of the sky, dun to turquoise, turquoise to deepest blue, pierced by the flaming sun, weighed hard and heavy on marching necks and shoulders.

Churchill was chosen to ride back from the cavalry advanced posts and report the position of the enemy, seen as a great black swathe on the plain of Omdurman, a small town not far from Khartoum. He rode back towards the infantry columns.

Soon I saw at their head a considerable cavalcade following a bright red banner. Drawing nearer I saw the Union Jack by the side of the Egyptian flag. Kitchener was riding alone two or three horses' lengths in front of his headquarters staff. His two standard bearers marched immediately behind him and the principal officers of the Anglo-Egyptian army staff followed in his train exactly as one would expect from the picture books.

He approached at an angle, reined in his horse slightly behind the pith-helmeted Sirdar riding his great white charger, and saluted.

He turned his grave face upon me. The heavy moustache, the queer rolling look of the eyes, the sunburnt almost purple cheeks and jowl made a vivid manifestation upon the senses [...] He listened in absolute silence to every word, our horses crunching the sand as we rode forward side by side.

There was a considerable pause before Kitchener replied. Some writers have speculated that he had recognised Churchill and was mastering his annoyance. More likely he was entirely preoccupied with the task in hand.

'You say the Dervish army is advancing. How long do you think I have got?'

Churchill blurted out, 'You have at least an hour—probably an hour and a half, sir, even if they come on at their present rate.'

Kitchener tossed his head, then bowed to indicate that Churchill's mission was discharged. Churchill reined in his horse and let the retinue flow past. Had he been right in his calculation? He was never good at sums, and he began to work out speeds and distances rather anxiously, 'in order to see whether my precipitate answer conformed to reason'. He was not far out. This was the first meeting of the two great men—one already famous, the other about to become so—and both destined to play parts in world history neither could have imagined.

Why had Kitchener objected to Churchill? To begin with, there were quite enough journalists on his staff, and Churchill had a commission from *The Morning Post*. Many other serving officers with aristocratic connections were doubling up as correspondents for newspapers like *The Times* and *The Daily Telegraph*. He did not want another scion of the silver-spooned classes scribbling criticisms at his elbow, particularly one known to be as pushy as Churchill was, but with certain individual journalists whose work he respected Kitchener had an excellent relationship. These included G. W. Steevens of the *Daily Mail* who had revealed the hopeless quality of marching boots supplied by the War Office, many of which had fallen apart in the desert sand causing men to go lame. Another was the Hon. Hubert Howard, correspondent for *The Times* and *The New York Herald*, who was killed by 'friendly fire' when a shell from a naval gunboat exploded close by whilst he and Kitchener were inspecting the vast dome of the Mahdi's tomb in Omdurman. However, Kitchener's famous comment to journalists waiting for news outside his tent on the day before the battle perhaps sums up his attitude to the press pack—'Get out of my way, you drunken swabs!' How would he have dealt with the media scrum of today, with its intrusive cameras, microphones and 'social media'?

The army, stretching three miles across the desert, was quickly concentrated into a defensive arc with its back against the River Nile and the protecting guns of the naval escort. Men were fed as soon as they came into the camp, and a zeriba (protective enclosure) of thorn bushes was interlocked around the perimeter in expectation of immediate attack. The gunboats on the Nile, and the British artillery on the opposite bank, began to fire a hail of shells in the direction of the Dervish army and the city of Omdurman, where the dome of the Mahdi's tomb, gleaming white in the sunshine, made an excellent range finder. But the Dervish army stopped. No attack came that day or during the night, despite fears that the Dervishes might favour an attack in darkness when the modern Maxim machine guns and artillery of the Anglo-Egyptian host would be negated by the inability to make out a target.

The Khalifa was experiencing mixed counsels from his Emirs, and it was not until 6.30 a.m. the following day, after Churchill had been in the saddle and scouting the surrounding hills since before dawn, that the Dervish host swept forward, a flashing sea of glittering steel and waving banners of white and yellow. 'A deadened roar came up to us in waves. They think they are going to win!' A division of 6,000 Dervishes moved onto the crest of a ridge and suddenly came under fire from the big guns.

> I saw the full blast of death strike this human wall. Down went their standards by dozens and their men by hundreds. Wide gaps and shapeless heaps appeared in their array. But none turned back. They all advanced towards our zeriba, opening a heavy rifle fire which wreathed them in smoke.

Churchill and his patrol rode back into the zeriba at full speed just before the infantry opened up on the Dervishes who were racing towards the perimeter.

Kitchener had taken up position on a knoll in the centre of his defensive arc behind the Cameron Highlanders, from where he began to direct operations. Once his forty Maxim machine guns opened up, along with the concentrated rifle fire of the infantry and the pounding artillery, the Dervish attack wavered and thinned out. Acres of human dead and dying lay before the zeriba, none of the men in the two converging attacks having reached any closer than 300 yards. The Dervishes carried mainly spears and swords, with a sprinkling of riflemen amongst their ranks. These now lay prone and fired at the defenders, inflicting some casualties. Another major attack came from the right, but the shouting enthusiasts bravely met the same fate. Many of the younger officers and men in Kitchener's army were experiencing for the first time the devastating power of modern defensive weapons, which would become all too familiar to them in the Great War.

With thousands of the enemy already dead and with his army intact, Kitchener decided he would move out of the zeriba and try to take Omdurman before the Khalifa fell back to defensive positions there. This is where he nearly came unstuck, as it was exactly what the Dervish leader wanted. His men were hidden in defiles and gulleys all over the plain of Omdurman, waiting for the infidel army to be strung out on the march. Churchill and the 21st Lancers were sent ahead to reconnoitre the ground, and as the main army laboriously followed them the cavalrymen ran into rifle fire from what appeared to be a handful of Dervishes occupying a dried-up watercourse.

Because of his bad shoulder, Churchill sheathed his sword and pulled out his pistol. The 21st Lancers turned to charge, but found they had run into the midst of a couple of thousand concealed troops. 'I was riding a handy sure-footed grey Arab polo pony.' Churchill guided his pony, and 'the clever animal dropped like a cat onto the sandy bed of the watercourse ... I found myself surrounded by dozens of men.' Some riders were brought to a standstill, dragged from their horses, speared and hacked to death. Others, like Churchill himself, rode through the throng and re-formed on the other side, lightly wounded or even untouched, as he was.

> Suddenly a Dervish sprang up in our midst [and] staggered towards me raising his spear. I shot him at less than a yard. He fell on the sand and lay there dead. How easy to kill a man! But I did not worry about it.

Churchill reloaded and asked his sergeant how he liked the charge. The man replied, 'Well, I don't exactly say I enjoyed it, sir, but I'll get more used to it next time!' At this the whole troop, who had looked serious, laughed out loud.

As Kitchener's army of 25,000 were strung out on the march towards Omdurman, leaving their baggage and wounded to be guarded by the gunboats, a gap opened between the main army and the rearguard division under the command of Gen. Hector Macdonald. Seeing a chance, thousands of Baggara Dervish cavalry were unleashed on Macdonald's brigade. An eyewitness described the scene:

> They evidently intended to break through our lines and divert our fire so as to give their infantry an opening. [...] It meant riding to certain death, but they galloped forward in loose open order, their ranks presenting one long ridge of flashing swords. Every soldier in the Sirdar's army watched breathlessly during this daring feat. Nearer

and nearer they came until the foremost horseman emerged almost within 200 yards of Macdonald's lines. A continuous stream of bullets from our lines was emptying the saddles but they came on until not a horseman was left. One Baggara succeeded in getting within thirty yards of the lines before he fell. The whole of the Dervish cavalry had been annihilated. There is no instance in history of a more superb devotion to a cause, or a greater contempt for death.

This was but the prelude to a display of equally reckless courage on the part of the Dervish infantry. The latter, though they had seen the fate of their cavalry, swept like a great white-crested wave towards our ranks, without the slightest pause or hesitation. The carnage was fearful, as the dauntless fanatics hurled themselves to inevitable death. The Emir Yacoub bore forward the great black banner of the Khalifa, his brother, surrounded by his relations and devoted followers. They surged forward until only a mere handful remained, and these never faltering, rushed onwards until they dropped dead beneath it.

Meanwhile, Kitchener deployed his brigades as if they were companies, switching them about, using his aides-de-camp as messengers to the brigade commanders who were fending off attacks from all sides, but at 11.30 a.m. the Dervish attacks were called off and they began to stream back towards the city. They had discovered that probing for a weak point was merely decimating their troops. The Khalifa tried to rally the townsfolk, but they were unwilling to sacrifice their town, their homes and their families to a lost cause. Instead, he paused at the shelled wreckage of the Mahdi's great tomb, prayed silently, then rode into the desert with his chosen followers. The bitter pill he had just swallowed was to be force fed again and again to the armies of the European powers when in turn their generals saw the flower of their youth scythed down and decimated by machine guns and high explosives in hopeless attacks.

A young hussar, Capt. Douglas Haig, newly attached to the Egyptian cavalry, himself a product of Army Staff College training and initially enthusiastic for Kitchener and his methods, criticised the lack of tactical planning before the battle. He believed that high casualties during the earlier battle of Atbara could have been avoided by more concentrated artillery and machine-gun fire. At Omdurman, Kitchener had 'spread out his force, thereby risking the destruction of a brigade. He seemed to have no plan, or tactical idea, for beating the enemy beyond allowing the latter to attack the camp.' Haig was to demonstrate both his own tactical abilities and deficiencies in the Great War.

Kitchener made a stately progress, riding his white charger into Omdurman in the midst of his two favourite Highland regiments, the Camerons and Seaforths. The town of mud houses appeared to be empty apart from an old man, an Emir, riding a donkey, who dismounted, prostrated himself before the Sirdar and presented the keys of the town. Kitchener told him there would be no massacre if all weapons were handed over promptly. Sporadic firing from the wounded and stragglers of the Dervish army led to reprisals, however, which were strongly criticised by Churchill. He wrote to his mother, 'I shall merely say that the victory of Omdurman was disgraced by the inhuman slaughter of the wounded, and that Kitchener was responsible for this.' To be fair, Kitchener could not be everywhere on the battlefield, and his troops when they met resistance were taking revenge on their fearsome enemies. But there was no wholesale massacre of townsfolk, who soon appeared on the streets, including thousands of Dervish women cooks and concubines.

The concept of humanely conducted warfare had been kicked in the teeth by Napoleon at the end of the eighteenth century when he 'brilliantly overturned' the established rules of war (and also by many other commanders before and since). In fact, such concepts dated from classical antiquity and the wars of ancient Greece. They were revived by the medieval rules of chivalry, but had only ever been practised between gentlemen of opposing sides. Common soldiers were routinely pillaged and butchered, even by their own countrymen after they had surrendered, as in the English Civil Wars of the seventeenth century. In the wars of the twentieth century, the conduct of warriors was reprised again.

Kitchener ordered the remains of the Mahdi to be exhumed from his splendid tomb and flung into the Nile and for the tomb itself to be demolished. His skull was presented to the Sirdar, who contemplated using it as an inkwell, according to Churchill, but kept it meanwhile in a kerosene can—a controversy for the newspaper correspondents to publicise to the world in outrage. They all approved of his memorial service for the murdered General Gordon, however, which was held in the overgrown ruins of the Governor's Palace in Khartoum a little further up the Nile. To everyone's astonishment, the usually imperturbable Kitchener was seen openly weeping, with tears rolling down his tanned cheeks at the singing of the hymn 'Abide with Me'. He was remembering his own unsuccessful part in attempts to relieve the city all those years before.

And what of the butcher's bill? About 11,000 Dervishes lay dead on the plain, and others among the ruins of Omdurman; 16,000 were prisoners, many of whom re-enlisted in the Egyptian Army. Of the Anglo-Egyptian host, forty-eight had been killed including twenty-three British, and 434 were wounded. The Sirdar thanked the Lord of Hosts for the victory bought at such little cost in British blood. When all the modern rifles, machine guns and artillery were concentrated in the hands of one side, this was to be expected. In the next war, in South Africa, Kitchener and Churchill had a foretaste of the doom to come.

# 5

# Goodbye Dolly Gray

'But,' she asked, 'you were glad that we won?'

'We didn't win!' was the emphatic reply of David Lloyd George to Frances Stevenson's enquiry about his attitude to the war in South Africa. In Lloyd George's opinion, it was not a victory at all but defeat disguised as a victory. His assessment of the result years later throws an interesting perspective on the conventional view:

> We had to give them back their land to rule and whereas they had ruled the Transvaal and the Orange Free State they were given in addition Cape Colony and Natal to rule [...] had we not done so, Botha and the others would have gone back to their farms, and waited for the moment to drive us from South Africa. We didn't win the Boer War!

He was not alone in this view. An English settler wrote:

> Not a single Boer I have ever met, or ever heard of, admits that the English were victorious. We left them unbeaten, we then treated them with ridiculous magnanimity which they interpreted as weakness or fear and worst blunder of all we agreed to give the fullest official rights to their language [...] now everything is Dutch.

The Boers certainly regarded South Africa as their country. They were born there and their ancestors had fought for and farmed the land for ten generations since the seventeenth century, when the first settlers arrived from Holland and Germany. Britain only got a toehold during the Napoleonic Wars and then purchased the rights to the Cape Colony. The Boers clashed with the British administration over the use on their farms and in the mines of black labour, who had no civic rights; when diamonds and later gold were discovered along the borders of the Boer 'free states'—where they had trekked to avoid British interference—it all got out of hand. Outlanders flooded in to get rich quick, and when they demanded equal political rights, Sir Alfred Milner for the British government used it as a pretext for an ultimatum to war.

The jingoistic hysteria in Britain against the perceived threat to Empire was initially very strong; even the Liberals supported the Tory government in the main, and only Labour stood apart for pacifism, but it was then a minority party with little influence. Throughout the war, Lloyd George spoke strongly against it, and as things went from bad to worse he argued that Britain needed to broaden its overseas policy to create an empire based on colonial independence and self rule. Liberal imperialists like Asquith, the future premier, were shocked by flaws in British social fabric highlighted by the wretched physical quality of Army recruits, due to poor diet and bad housing of the working classes. Between 40 and 60 per cent of potential recruits were found to be unfit. The Liberals determined to support Lloyd George's ideas for a radical taxation policy to tackle poverty and urban decay. Almost alone, crying against the howling gale of war fever to begin with, he eventually came to represent a broad consensus of opinion in a Liberal Party strongly poised for power.

Lines from the popular song 'Goodbye Dolly Gray' summed up the enthusiasm at the outbreak of war:

*Goodbye Dolly, I must leave you, though it breaks my heart to go.*
*Something tells me I am needed at the front to fight the foe!*

Sadly, the song tells that the young man did not return but fell 'with his face to the foe'—a fate all too frequent among the soldiers sent to be deployed in outdated tactics against expert marksmen armed with modern smokeless Mauser rifles and Krupp guns, who knew how to use the lie of the land to hide themselves from their enemy.

No one was more enthusiastic than Winston Churchill. 'I thought it very sporting of the Boers to take on the whole British Empire, and I felt quite glad they were not defenceless and had put themselves in the wrong by making preparations.' He jumped at the offer of covering the operations as war correspondent for *The Morning Post* at an inflated salary and with all expenses paid. Having earlier resigned his commission in the Army, he was free to move wherever he liked and was soon on board the *Dunnottar Castle* steaming for South Africa with Gen. Sir Redvers Buller, the newly appointed commander-in-chief.

In later years, and with hindsight, he was to write:

Never believe any war will be smooth and easy, or that anyone who embarks on that strange voyage can measure the tides and hurricanes he will encounter [...] however sure you are that you can easily win, there would not be a war if the other man did not think he also had a chance.

So it proved. The initial disasters were all on the British side before Buller even set foot on African soil—and when he did, things did not improve. An early disaster for Churchill was the unfortunate loss in his share of a consignment of choice wines shipped out by his father's old friend Lord Gerard, and labelled 'Castor Oil' to lessen the likelihood of pilfering. At Durban this urgently required medication was redirected to the hospitals where doubtless it did a power of good! Churchill's own supply of sixty bottles of wines and spirits was considered 'quite modest' by his biographer Roy Jenkins, himself a celebrated wine-bibber, who thought these were just for the voyage out! No wonder Churchill was sick as a dog as he made his way to Natal aboard a pitching tramp steamer in an Antarctic gale. In a small bunk below decks:

> I lay in extreme physical misery while our tiny ship bounded and reeled, kicked and pitched, and fell and turned almost over and righted itself again, hour after hour through an endless afternoon, a still longer evening and an eternal night.

A memory he said he would take engraved on his mind 'to the catacombs of age'.

At Estcourt he took up quarters in an empty bell tent pitched in the shunting yard at the railway station with the correspondents of *The Times* and *The Manchester Guardian*. He was immediately invited to accompany an armoured train that was to scout the country ahead, commanded by an acquaintance from the Tirah expedition, Capt. Aylmer Haldane. 'Nothing looks more formidable and impressive than an armoured train; but nothing is in fact more vulnerable and helpless.' This was quickly proven fourteen miles down the track when the leading three carriages were suddenly blown off the rails. The stricken train, derailed in sections, was under continuous bombardment from mushroom-like shrapnel airbursts and rifle fire that rattled against the armour plating of the carriages containing the soldiers. Churchill ran to the engine while Haldane directed the rear naval gun and the soldiers to hold off the Boer attack. The soldiers in the front carriages were dazed and injured, and a shrapnel burst suddenly wounded the engine driver, who sprang from his cab complaining that he wasn't paid to be shot at.

Churchill's natural qualities of courage and leadership exerted themselves immediately. The driver was only lightly wounded in the face by a splinter of metal and Churchill was able to calm him amidst the fusillade of shot and persuade him that their only hope lay in getting the remaining carriages away. The driver remounted the cab and Churchill directed him to shunt a derailed carriage that was partially blocking the line out of the way. Eventually the engine set off under fire, carrying the wounded packed in every available cranny, with the uninjured infantry running alongside, eventually falling behind as the engine gathered speed. Churchill jumped from the train to run back to them, but was cut off by Boer marksmen. All the remaining soldiers on foot were captured and Churchill found himself a prisoner of war, correspondent status notwithstanding. Fortunately, he had left his Mauser pistol in the cab of the engine in the excitement and was quietly disposing of the clips of ammunition he carried in his pockets when his captor demanded, 'What have you got there?' He held out his hand. 'What is it?' Winston asked innocently. 'I picked it up.' The Boer examined the unfamiliar clip then threw it away.

After three days' marching, including a detour around the Boer lines besieging Ladysmith where the sound of guns rumbled continuously, the prisoners, several officers including Haldane and Churchill, and fifty men, arrived at Pretoria where the officers were confined in the State Model School. Here Churchill experienced about a month of captivity, 'when days were very long and hours crawled like paralytic centipedes'. He demanded his release on the grounds that he was a non-combatant. In fact, the Boers were secretly debating releasing him when he seized the initiative. The Natal newspapers had praised his actions in getting the engine away with the wounded, but some pro-Boer commentators were suggesting that he had violated his neutral status. One even implied that he ought to be shot! Anyway, tired of awaiting a propitious moment to escape, he launched himself one evening from the cubicle of an outside toilet over the wall of the State Model School compound. As he later described it, 'I leapt from a water closet and into the pages of history.'

Subsequently Captain Haldane and a Lieutenant Brockie claimed that he was supposed to wait for the right moment so that they could escape together, but Churchill just saw an opportunity when the guards were distracted and grabbed it. This was very typical of his decisive one-man-band attitude, as well as his impetuosity. He strolled out through the darkened town and jumped onto a goods train pulling out of the station, with some difficulty because of his dislocated shoulder, secreting himself among some coal bags. About eighty miles down the track he leapt off and wandered about in a confused manner with no clear plan, until in desperation he knocked on the door of a house near some mine workings. With incredible luck, he had found the only Englishman for miles.

Mr John Howard, manager of the Transvaal Collieries, turned out to be a good friend. With the aid of other British workers, including Mr Daniel Dewsnap, a stout miner from Oldham, he was wound down into the mine workings, where he spent several days on a mattress reading newspapers and the novel *Kidnapped* by candlelight, attended only by the other mine residents, a tribe of white rats, that ran over him as he slept and tried to eat his candles!

Mr Howard brought him a poster that had been circulated. It read in Dutch and English: '£25 to anyone who brings the escaped prisoner of war CHURCHILL dead or alive to this office.' As Winston had £75 in his pocket he still felt comparatively safe. Eventually his departure in a space made between wool bales on a train bound for Portuguese East Africa was arranged, and Mr Dewsnap squeezed his hand in a powerful grip, whispering providentially, 'They'll all vote for you next time!' Churchill had already stood unsuccessfully as a parliamentary candidate in the Oldham constituency but was hoping for another go. The merchant to whom the bales belonged, Charles Burnham, a local storekeeper, travelled on the train and kept watch, dispensing bribes to speed up delays, and after several days the train crossed the border. A gleeful Churchill roused the British Consul in Lourenço Marques to announce his successful escape.

While Churchill was receiving an avalanche of publicity and giving an impromptu speech on the steps of the Town Hall at Durban (he loved an audience), Kitchener had received an urgent message in Cairo that he was needed to save the Empire. Things were going badly in the South African War, earning the commander the nickname of 'Sir Reverse Buller'. Churchill, fresh from his escape, had rushed back to ask Buller for a lieutenant's commission in the South African Light Horse, which he was given, as well as his continued *Morning Post* correspondent status. So he was present at the blood letting of Spion Kop, where entire British regiments were decimated by artillery on a barren hilltop while the generals did little to support them. It was found that Boer guns had greater range and power than those of the professional army. Churchill described his respected enemy as a terrible adversary. 'The individual Boer, mounted in suitable country, is worth from three to five regular soldiers.' He advocated either better quality troopers to fight them or overwhelming numbers. 'There is plenty of work here for a quarter of a million men.'

Kitchener wired from Cairo, suggesting the types of artillery needed:

All our field guns were originally 12-pounders; they were then bored out to make 15-pounders, which naturally only allows there being fired with reduced charges. We are hopelessly behind the age, owing to our artillery officers' dislike of anything new.

He raced to join the new commander-in-chief, Lord Roberts, en route in the *Dunnottar Castle* at Gibraltar and sailed for Cape Town as his chief of staff and second-in-command of the army. Sizing up the situation, Roberts and Kitchener quickly decided to march their fresh army from the Cape across the Orange Free State to take the stronghold of Bloemfontein and then on to Pretoria in the Transvaal. Kitchener briefed the cavalry commanders General French and his chief of staff Douglas Haig that they were to ride on ahead, find a way through the enemy with their 3,000 horsemen and relieve the besieged town of Kimberley while the juggernaut of Roberts' 25,000-strong infantry followed on. They were told that the future of the Empire rested on their shoulders.

The Boer commander facing them, Gen. Pieter Cronje, was taken by surprise and started to withdraw once Kimberley was relieved by French and Haig. But the dust raised by his ox wagons was spotted by Kitchener as he stood on a kopje (rocky hill) scanning the countryside through binoculars. His long years campaigning in Africa had honed his bushcraft skills, and like the desert nomads he knew so well, he had developed an instinct for war. Columns of infantry were soon in pursuit, Kitchener once more ordering French with his best men to ride ahead of the Boers and cut them off. Despite their previous exertions, the 1,500 cavalrymen rode like the wind, dragging a battery of field guns with them. As Cronje and his 5,000 men were about to cross the Modder River they unexpectedly came under fire from French's twelve field guns that threw shells into the midst of Cronje's position and denied a river passage. The leading British infantry also began to arrive and open fire on the beleaguered Boers, who had their women and baggage wagons with them. Cronje withdrew into a defensive laager above the steep rocky banks of the river at Paardeberg Drift.

Kitchener's forces started to arrive piecemeal and badly co-ordinated, his recent reorganisation of their transport and supply system now resulting in confusion and inefficiency at a vital moment. The Boers were expecting reinforcements too and were in a strong position, but Kitchener, against the advice of more experienced generals, decided on a rapid assault. This had worked for him in the attack on Atbara in the Sudan, but here he was facing a redoubtable and well-armed enemy. Having made an early morning reconnaissance of the Boer defences, he looked at his watch and said, 'It is now seven o'clock. We shall be in the laager by half past ten.' He ordered a frontal assault by Lt Gen. Kelly Kenny, who candidly thought Kitchener mad, supported by attacks on the right and left, including one across the river by the Highlanders, which Kitchener then countermanded in mid-stream. He rode backwards and forwards across the battlefield, personally shouting orders like the Duke of Wellington, but without the Duke's calm understatement, or apparently any clear idea of strategy or even what was happening.

The other generals were convinced that the highly excited Lord Kitchener of Khartoum (he had been ennobled after Omdurman) did not know what he was doing. Despite artillery bombardments on the laager, no British unit managed to get within 300 yards of the Boer trenches. It was like Omdurman, only the other way round. The Highland Brigade was pinned down by fire beneath the bank of the river, and Col. Hannay of the mounted infantry was ordered by Kitchener to ride up to the laager and fire into it. He took fifty volunteers, knowing the futility of the action, and rode at full pelt almost to the defences before he and his men were all needlessly sacrificed, falling in a hail of bullets.

By day's end the Boers were still in position; there were 1,200 British casualties, and Kitchener's army was also under fire from Christian De Wet's guerrillas, who had ridden up to the south and occupied a hill. Short of rations and medical supplies, the British position was grim when the commander-in-chief, 67-year-old Lord Roberts, arrived the following day to view the shambles. Having spoken to the other commanders and hearing their accounts of Kitchener's handling of the battle, Roberts discontinued frontal assaults but kept up the artillery bombardments. He sent Kitchener on a mission to repair bridges and railway lines near Colesberg. After enduring a week of bombardment, and running short of ammunition and supplies, Cronje surrendered, giving Roberts the first major British victory of the war. Despite the Modder River being contaminated by the bodies of the dead, it was used as drinking water, so that cases of typhoid soon outnumbered casualties from the battle. The victory had come at a high price and had slowed Roberts' drive for Bloemfontein and Pretoria.

Why had Kitchener acted so rashly? One reason was that he found himself temporarily in supreme command while Roberts was delayed by illness. He was no doubt anxious to grab a quick victory so that his name would again be covered in glory. On this occasion his instinct to assault the Boer position immediately was wrong. By nature autocratic and stubborn, having made a mistake he did not know how to extricate himself or his troops without losing face. He was a slow learner, but he learned his lessons well. His own explanation of the action was that 'war means risks and you cannot play the game and always win; and the sooner those in authority realise this, the better'.

But it was a victory. The news so heartened Buller's men far to the north that they too pushed forward and liberated Ladysmith from besieging forces. On 16 May 1900, the relief of Mafeking, defended by Col. Baden Powell (of later boy scout fame) for 217 days with a couple of thousand armed police and natives, caused rejoicing throughout the Empire and consternation among the Boers. They fell back in confusion, with flagging morale. Bloemfontein, Johannesburg and Pretoria surrendered in quick succession, and the presidents of the two republics, Kruger and Steyn, fled. The Boer practice of taking women and children along with them to look after the ox wagons had proved a mistake.

Another disaster nearly engulfed Kitchener while his train was resting in sidings near Heilbron Road station on the night of 12/13 June. The Boers having decided to carry on the war with guerrilla tactics, a strong force led by Piet De Wet attacked in the night, surprising the fifty mounted infantrymen supposed to be protecting the slumbering general. Kitchener sprang up in his pyjamas and with the help of his staff got a horse ready in one of the carriages, swung into the saddle and, as the doors were dragged open, leapt from the train and galloped off into the night. He made it to a nearby Yeomanry camp, but his bodyguard had all been taken prisoner. Another blow to his prestige.

Churchill meanwhile had become a roving correspondent again and cycled through Johannesburg in civilian clothes just as the Boers were retreating from the city. He reached Roberts' army on the other side without mishap. Shortly after, he went with his cousin, the young Duke of Marlborough, who was an officer on Roberts' staff, and took the surrender of the British internment camp commanders in Pretoria, having the satisfaction of liberating his former fellow prisoners:

> While the last of the guard stood uncertain what to do, the long penned up officers surrounded them and seized their weapons. Someone produced a Union Jack and the first British flag was hoisted over Pretoria!

It seemed as if the war had reached a successful conclusion, and towards the end of the year Lord Roberts handed command over to Kitchener and headed home to general rejoicings in London. But the Boer guerrillas had not given up and Kitchener, now commander-in-chief, had the chance to prove himself at last. Churchill had also gone home, and in the so-called 'khaki election' was returned as MP for Oldham, having fought on the platform that the war was just and necessary and that the

Liberal pro-Boers had been wrong to oppose it. In the Theatre Royal, Oldham, where Churchill described his escape to a vast enthusiastic audience, on mentioning the help of Dan Dewsnap, who had wound him down the coal mine, the audience shouted, 'His wife's in the gallery!' There was a cry of general jubilation. Lionised wherever he went, Churchill was supported by fellow speakers Joseph Chamberlain (the Colonial Secretary and the leading imperialist of the government, who was the idol of the moment) and Arthur Balfour (soon to be Prime Minister). 'For three weeks I had what seemed a triumphal progress through the country. I was 26. Was it wonderful that I should have thought I had arrived?'

Meanwhile, out on the arid veldt very different emotions were animating the remaining Boer commandos. Terror and counter-terror were becoming commonplace. Kitchener had begun to exercise his implacable military mind on the problems of containment in the vast tracts of landscape over which the Boer horsemen ranged freely, attacking an outpost here and decimating a column of troops there, then riding off into the limitless territory. Unlike the British, they knew every waterhole, each obscure drift or river crossing, and all the secret passes through the rocky hills. They could also gain support and succour from the farmhouses of the veldt.

Kitchener got out his engineer's pen and compass, slide rule and set square, and poring over maps and plans he devised a methodical scheme that was cruel, calculated and effective. By late 1901, South African railways were shadowed by long lines of blockhouses manned by soldiers, both black and white, and linked by barbed wire. Large tracts of the veldt were also subdivided by the blockhouse system, and all the succour-giving farms had been depopulated and burned. Up to 140,000 men, women and children were incarcerated in thirty-four internment camps, where water-borne diseases killed at least a third. Kitchener also created large mobile columns of mounted infantry to sweep the wired-off tracts, and employed 'joiners'—spies and renegades who were sick of the war and wanted it all to end and for everything to get back to normal. It was not easy, because he had formidable opponents: Gen. Jan Smuts conducted a brilliant campaign against the Cape Colony, and Christian De Wet escaped containment again and again, striking now here, now there, and defeating superior numbers of British.

Kitchener was denounced as Herod by Lloyd George for causing the deaths of children in the camps, which had been visited and reported on by Emily Hobhouse, a Christian welfare campaigner, who blamed Kitchener for the appalling conditions. However, he was not entirely to blame, as knowledge of hygiene was rudimentary among veldt-dwelling Boer farmers who normally lived quite isolated lives. But basic necessities like adequate food and water, soap and sufficient tents were not provided in the bare camps, and children died like the flies that infested everything in the stifling heat.

It was around this time that the curious incident of the starlings occurred, which perhaps gives a psychological insight into Kitchener's solitary emotions. His young

ADC, Frank Maxwell, described how the commander-in-chief was found one morning rushing around the room in his dressing gown, chasing a couple of young starlings that had fallen down the chimney. Placed in the pigeon house in the garden, one soon died and Maxwell pleaded in vain for the release of the second bird, which he claimed was too young to eat the proffered worms and titbits placed before it. In addition, the parents had appeared and were clamouring for its release! When this bird eventually escaped its guards, a hue and cry ensued and the commander-in-chief was not satisfied until it was safe behind wire again. 'I've never been so fond of that bird since it's been loose,' remarked a garden-soiled and breathless Kitchener, who then spent considerable time chirping at it through the wire and watching it eat worms. 'The operations in South Africa received no attention for most of the rest of the day,' commented Maxwell.

In fact, Kitchener had many grave issues to decide upon. Over 400 Cape Colony rebels who had supported the Boers were under sentence of death, but Kitchener commuted most sentences to imprisonment and only forty-four of the most aggravated cases led to execution. Controversially, he also signed the death warrant of Lt Breaker Morant, an Australian officer in the Bushveldt Carbineers, convicted of killing Boer prisoners and the murder of a pro-Boer clergyman.

In March 1902, when Kitchener was hopeful of bringing the Boer leaders to the negotiating table, a force of about a thousand British soldiers under Lord Methuen was defeated in a running battle and lost their artillery and stores after surrendering. Maxwell recorded:

> It floored poor K. and he didn't appear at five meals. On the morning of his recovery he volunteered the remark that his 'nerves had all gone to pieces' but after eating a very, for him, sound breakfast, that was the end of the slump in his spirits.

Although nearly half a million white soldiers from throughout the Empire served against the Boers in the South African War, with their numbers augmented by local blacks, only 78,000 Boers opposed them and never more than 47,000 at one time. Ultimately only about 20,000 were left in the field, and arms, morale and hope were running low. Native blacks were increasingly fighting for the British, a worrying development for the Boer farmers. Despite this, superior Boer tactics defeated British units again and again. When cornered miles from assistance, British soldiers readily surrendered and officers had difficulty preventing this happening, as the Boers simply relieved the men of their boots, trousers and weapons before contemptuously setting them free and riding off into the veldt with captured horses. 'Hang this wretched surrendering,' wrote Maxwell, who had won a VC in a recent action. 'Though I suppose sitting in an armchair it's easy to be brave; but it does seem to happen a bit often, doesn't it?'

Finally, Kitchener managed to get the leaders Botha, De Wet, De la Rey and Smuts to discuss terms for a cessation of hostilities. His efforts were blocked by the ambitious Milner, who fancied himself as the new Viceroy of South Africa and was demanding a complete surrender. Although Milner was the politician, it was Kitchener who exhibited the greatest flexibility in recognising the realities of the situation. Back in London, Lloyd George criticised Milner as 'a man who strolled among his orchids' miles from the action, while Kitchener was 'a soldier who knew what war meant; he strove to make peace'. But peace came at a price. Kitchener intimated to Smuts that a new Liberal government would probably grant self rule to the Boer republics whatever the current government said, and on this basis, and to end the suffering of their families in the camps, the Boers signed an agreement.

The South African War was over at a cost of £200 million, several billions today, and 22,000 British casualties, with a similar number of Boer deaths in the field but mainly in the camps—a cruel but effective factor in bringing the process to a conclusion. Britain's reputation in defending its Empire had fallen in the eyes of the world. Queen Victoria was dead. A policy of splendid isolation was reprised and abandoned as new alliances were sought with France and Russia, which inevitably drew Britain and its Empire to the burning ground of an Armageddon, now beginning to loom menacingly from the growing ambition of the central European powers of Germany and Austria-Hungary.

# 6

# Countdown to Armageddon

*Far I hear the steady drummer, drumming like a noise in dreams;*
*Far and near, and low and louder, on the roads of earth go by;*
*Dear to friends and food for powder, soldiers marching, all to die.*
A Shropshire Lad

Young Germany was a latecomer to the scramble for imperial possessions overseas, having become a united nation under Bismarck only in the mid-nineteenth century. With his creation of the Kaiser, (literally Caesar—emperor) the King of Prussia was raised to become Emperor of Germany, after an economic alliance and then military domination of the German federation of small principalities. Austria-Hungary, its only rival, had been humiliated by defeat in the 1860s, its ageing empire becoming the junior partner in the Berlin-led foreign policy making of the Wilhelmstrasse, named after the little Kaiser with big ambitions. (Wilhelm II was about 5 feet 7 inches tall, the same height as Churchill and Lloyd George.) German diplomacy was marked by clumsy attempts to bully and browbeat older and more established empires. It had worked with Austria and then France. Why not again with others?

There was much for Germany to be jealous of and greedy about. Britain and France had massive overseas colonial empires and were still acquiring territory. British overseas assets totalled £4 billion in 1914, twice that of France, the nearest competitor, and almost as much as the investments of all the other major powers (including the US) put together. The British fleet that guarded its maritime empire was kept at a strength that made it equal in force to its two nearest naval rivals. After Bismarck's exit from power, the posturing at the Wilhelmstrasse convinced British ministers that Germany intended to dominate Europe. The Anglo-French Entente, an expression of solidarity in the face of German aggression, was the first result in 1904. Three years later, differences with Russia were patched up when the Triple Entente between Britain, Russia and France was formed. This alarmed Germany, but it was entirely its own fault, as its machinations had provoked the response. In 1905, German threats forced France to sacrifice the minister who had negotiated the agreement with Britain, but at a conference in Algeciras demanded by Germany, Britain stood uncompromisingly beside its ally and German aggression evaporated for the time being.

After his entry to Parliament as a Conservative MP for Oldham, Churchill had become disillusioned with his father's old party, finding it not quite as open to radicals as he had expected. He crossed the floor of the House on the question of Free Trade in 1904, going to sit (by prearrangement) with Lloyd George, who warmly welcomed him into the Liberal fold. Churchill's first job in the subsequent Liberal government was Under Secretary for the Colonies, followed by President of the Board of Trade. Taking his lead from the more experienced Lloyd George, Churchill leaned away from aggressive militarism and expenditure on armaments—at least to begin with.

On taking up his post, Churchill had appointed Edward Marsh, a young civil servant, as his private secretary. Marsh visited Lady Lytton (a former love interest of Churchill's) to get the low-down on his new boss. 'The first time you meet Winston,' she told him, 'you see all his faults, and the rest of your life you spend in discovering his virtues.' Churchill's own boss, Lord Elgin, was warned against his junior minister by a senior civil servant in the department:

> He is most tiresome to deal with and will give you trouble—as his father did—in any position to which he may be called. The restless energy, uncontrollable desire for notoriety and lack of moral perception make him an anxiety indeed!

Marsh had an early insight into Churchill's limited knowledge of the people whose votes he sought in Manchester. The two men were staying in the splendid, newly built, glazed-brick Midland Hotel near the city's St Peter's Square. Churchill suggested a walk and they quickly got into mean streets. Looking around at the sooty terraced rows, the young minister commented: 'Fancy living in one of these streets—never seeing anything beautiful—never eating anything savoury—never saying anything clever!' He probably did not appreciate at the time that his versatile, self-made colleague, Lloyd George, had been born in one of these selfsame sooty streets of Manchester.

Kitchener, after his African adventure, spent the 1900s reorganising the Indian Army and fighting a battle with the Viceroy, Lord Curzon, over the methods he was employing. Denied the crowning pinnacle of the Viceroyship of India when it became vacant, he took the huff and went on a world tour inspecting military forces. He was placated by becoming British Agent (Pro-Consul) in Cairo, his old boss Lord Cromer's former job. Here he truly enjoyed himself as 'El Gran Lord', as some Egyptians styled him, or less flatteringly perhaps, the Lloyd George of Egypt. He ruled as a Pharaoh with absolute power, but did all he could to develop the country he felt was his spiritual home and in which he had spent the greater part of his adult life. He was particularly assiduous in helping the Fellaheen peasants to a better life as well as promoting building projects, indulgently hosting grand dinners with feasting off solid gold plates, and collecting porcelain.

Lloyd George had survived as an MP despite his unpopularity during the Boer War. In Campbell-Bannerman's Liberal government he was given his first proper job as President of the Board of Trade and quickly proved that he was a competent administrator and negotiator as well as an efficient troublemaker! Acts reforming patents, shipping, ports and companies all rolled out under his seal. He was particularly good at solving labour disputes, utilising his Celtic charm to persuade railway owners to accept collective bargaining nationally and union leaders to lessen their demands. He was rewarded with the Chancellorship, and his People's Budget of 1909 drew a line in the sand. As he said, it would 'wage implacable warfare against poverty and squalidness'. Landowners would have to fork out to pay for both social development and the new Dreadnought-class battleships needed to offset the threat from Germany. The Lords went mad. His riposte was that they were only 'five hundred men chosen at random from among the unemployed'. The people loved it.

Meanwhile, there were straws, or rather sparks, blowing in the wind, warning of a future conflagration. The Kaiser had declared himself 'Admiral of the Atlantic.' Churchill pondered in his book *The World Crisis*: 'All sorts of sober minded people in England began to be profoundly disquieted. What did Germany want a great navy for? Against whom, except us, could she measure it, match it, or use it?' There was a deep and growing feeling, no longer confined to political or diplomatic circles, that the Prussians meant mischief, that they envied the splendour of the British Empire, and that if they saw a good chance at its expense, they would take full advantage of it.

> [...] in the space of five years Germany's policy and the growth of her armaments led her to arouse and alarm most profoundly three of the greatest powers in the world. Two of them, France and Russia, had been forced to bow to the German will by the plain threat of war. The third power—Britain—had also been made to feel that hands were being laid upon the very foundations of her existence. A German navy was coming into being at our very doors which must expose us to dangers only to be warded off by strenuous exertions and by a vigilance as tense as that of actual war.

After seeing the sinister preparations in Germany and watching army manoeuvres alongside the Kaiser, who was magnificently attired in his imperial uniform and eagle-crest helmet, Churchill commented privately, 'He wants to be like Napoleon, but he doesn't want to have to fight Napoleon's battles ... Instead he sends up puffs of smoke and glows from afar like a volcano.'

Lloyd George, soon after becoming Chancellor of the Exchequer in 1908, was invited by Foreign Secretary Sir Edward Grey to meet Count Metternich, the German ambassador in London. A discussion about Britain's misgivings over German naval programmes ensued, in which the ministers attempted to explain the British position without further discord. Lloyd George was considered by Metternich to belong to the British 'peace party' of the Liberal government. His report to the Kaiser (with marginal notes written by that august personage) showed the monarch's wilful misunderstanding of almost everything that was said by the British ministers. Despite Metternich's careful phrasing, the German emperor was determined to take offence, even at the idea that such a discussion could have taken place. In retrospect, it can only be understood as a manifestation of Germany's sensitivity to imagined slights as a young nation feeling its way in the world of established powers. The Kaiser certainly represented the feelings of many of his insecure countrymen and women, unlike the Germans of today, confident of their European pre-eminence.

On a trip to Germany later the same year, Lloyd George met the future wartime German Chancellor, Von Bethmann-Hollweg. 'He was very bitter about what he called the encirclement of Germany with an iron ring by France, Russia and England.' Lloyd George tried to reassure him of Britain's peaceful intent, but in the course of a dinner where large steins of lager were consumed Von Bethmann-Hollweg became very heated:

> 'An iron ring,' he repeated violently, shouting out the statement and waving his arm to the whole assembled company. 'England is embracing France. She is making friends with Russia. But it is not that you love each other. It is that you hate Germany!' And he repeated and shouted the word '*hate*' thrice.

The German leader was convinced that the British were also decadent. 'In England you go to your office at eleven, you have a long lunch, you leave at four. On Thursday you go to the country; you remain until Tuesday morning and call it a weekend!'

Lloyd George also described a scene at Stuttgart airport where a Zeppelin airship was to make a demonstration but had crashed and been destroyed. He wrote:

> Of course we were disappointed, but disappointment was a totally inadequate word for the agony of grief and dismay which swept over the massed Germans who witnessed the catastrophe. There was no loss of life to account for it. Hopes and ambitions far wider than those concerned with a scientific and mechanical success appeared to have shared the wreck of the dirigible. Then the crowd swung into the chanting of 'Deutschland uber Alles' with a fanatic fervour of patriotism. What spearpoint of imperial advance did this airship portend? These incidents were cracks in the cold surface through which the hot seething lava of unrest could be seen stirring uneasily underneath.

On his return to England, a profoundly disturbed Lloyd George presented a paper to the government outlining his ideas for a system of militia training on the continental model, which should have all-party backing as a matter of urgency:

> The submarine and the Zeppelin offered a possible challenge to the invincibility of our defence. I felt we should be safer in this country if we had a system of training for our

young manhood which would fit it for the defence of the Realm in the possible event of the invasion of our shores.

He argued that future inventions might neutralise the defensive powers of the Royal Navy and that Britain's tiny army was inadequate to resist the gigantic continental forces that existed in Europe, should this become necessary. He had even joked with Metternich, quoting the words of Prince Bismarck, that in the event of a landing of the British Army in Germany, Bismarck would have 'left it to the police to arrest the British corps'. The plan foundered upon a Conservative Party veto.

In the summer of 1911, a second Moroccan crisis between France and Germany blew up. This time the French had sent an expedition to Fez seeking to acquire territory, the Germans retaliating by ordering a gunboat to Agadir on the Moroccan coast. Britain's official letter to Berlin received no reply for over two weeks. Churchill, who by this time had become Home Secretary, urged his friend Lloyd George that something must be done to avert the drift towards war.

The result was a remarkable statement from the Chancellor in a Mansion House speech to bankers and businessmen of the City of London. 'I would make great sacrifices to preserve peace,' he began. But as the speech wore on, it was clear that the great radical Chancellor was in an uncompromising mood as he set out Britain's position over the current crisis so that there would be no possibility of misunderstanding. If surrender of our hard-won interests overseas and our place in the world were the price of peace, then 'peace at that price would be a humiliation intolerable for a great country like ours to endure'.

The Germans were furious. Churchill and Lloyd George were called to an emergency meeting with Sir Edward Grey, who had just sent to warn the fleet that it might be attacked at any minute. On behalf of the government he had defended Lloyd George's speech as moderate and entirely right, when ambassador Metternich protested and demanded an apology. The Kaiser was outraged and Metternich was summoned to return to Berlin. The effect was to concentrate Churchill's mind on matters of national security. He quickly discovered that the entire reserves of naval cordite were stored in magazines at Chattenden and Lodge Hill at Chatham, guarded by a few unarmed police constables. Realising that twenty determined German agents could at a stroke paralyse half the defensive power of the Royal Navy, he arranged for the police to be reinforced by soldiers and armed immediately.

All around flowed the busy life of peaceful unsuspecting easygoing Britain. The streets were thronged with men and women utterly devoid of any sense of danger from abroad. For a hundred years the safety of the homeland had never been threatened. They went about their business, their sport, year after year, generation after generation, in perfect confidence and considerable ignorance. All their ideas were derived from conditions of peace. All their arrangements were the result of long peace. Most of them would have been incredulous, many would have been very angry if they had been told that we might be near a tremendous war.

Churchill also reflected on the potential enemy:

Ah! foolish diligent Germans, working so hard, thinking so deeply, marching and counter-marching on the parade grounds of the Fatherland, poring over long calculations, fuming in new found prosperity, discontented amid the splendour of mundane success, how many bulwarks to your peace and glory did you not, with your own hands, successively tear down?

He had several times witnessed the might of Germany's armed forces at manoeuvres in the mid- to late 1900s. 'Wave after wave of valiant manhood ... the thousands of strong horses dragging cannon and great howitzers along the roads and up the ridges.'

Within three weeks he sat down and, almost unaided, composed a masterful memorandum describing the likely course of an imminent European conflict which he circulated to members of the Committee of Imperial Defence. With surprising prescience, he accurately (as it turned out) charted the early course of the war. Germany would attack through Belgium. Britain would send a force of 107,000 men, with another 100,000 from India arriving on the fortieth day, who would rebalance the scale and beat back the Germans before they delivered the knockout blow against the French Army. It more or less came to pass three years later, in September 1914 at the Battle of the Marne, one of the great turning points of military history. Churchill had accurately foreseen the future, but the future he saw was a dark one.

He himself was not dismayed. His new wife (he had recently married Clementine Hosier) was convinced that his main interest in the annual manoeuvres of the Oxford Yeomanry, of which he was an officer, was the opportunity for hard drinking and gambling that they afforded. But a letter the fledgling warlord sent to his lady love should have dispelled such thoughts. After one such weekend with the soldiers he wrote:

I would greatly like to have some practice in the handling of large forces. I have much confidence in my judgement on things [...] but on nothing do I seem to feel the truth more than in tactical combinations. It is a vain and foolish thing to say—but you will not laugh at it. I am sure I have the root of the matter in me.

Churchill was doubtless conscious of his biological inheritance from the great first Duke of Marlborough, whom Wellington had described as the perfect general. But, so far, the line from John Churchill to Winston Churchill had been devoid of military distinction.

In the meantime, Churchill was summoned to stay with Prime Minister Asquith at his Scottish retreat. On the way back from the golf links, Asquith asked him if he would like to go to the Admiralty as First Lord. 'Indeed I would,' Churchill replied with alacrity. 'The fading light of evening disclosed in the far distance the silhouettes of two battleships steaming slowly out of the Firth of Forth. They seemed invested with a new significance to me,' he wrote later. That night beside his bed he picked up a bible and read in Deuteronomy:

*Hear O Israel: thou art to pass over Jordan this day, to go in to possess nations greater and mightier than thyself, cities great and fenced up to heaven; a people great and tall, the children of the Anakims, whom thou knowest, and of whom thou hast heard say, 'Who can stand before the children of Anak'. Understand therefore this day, that the Lord thy God is he which goeth over before thee; as a consuming fire he shall destroy them, and he shall bring them down before thy face.*

It seemed a message full of reassurance to Churchill in his new task.

The Liberal Party was not happy with all this talk of war and naval estimates. Early in 1912, the National Liberal Federation voted in favour of retrenchment and reform in preference to Dreadnoughts. The vulnerability of these monster ships was brought into question when the newly launched *Titanic*, a White Star passenger liner and hailed as unsinkable, sank on its maiden voyage across the Atlantic with massive loss of life. R.B. Haldane, who had been Churchill's rival for the Admiralty post, was quietly dispatched to Germany to try and reach a compromise about the naval arms race. Fluent in German, having been educated at Göttingen, he was a good choice, and had already carried out a reform of the War Office with Douglas Haig to create an Imperial General Staff, and co-ordinated war plans. The discussions dragged on inconclusively, Asquith commenting:

Nothing, I believe, will meet Germany's purpose which falls short of a promise on our part of neutrality; a promise we cannot give. And she makes no firm or solid offer, even in exchange for that.

About this time, Britain nearly lost its best military personality when, in July 1912, Kitchener came close to assassination. Egypt, always volatile and simmering with nationalist tides of resentment against foreign rule, had already thrown up leaders striving for independence from both Ottoman Turkey and Imperialist Britain (supposedly 'looking after the shop' for the country). A nationalist, Taher Arabi, burst through the crowds surrounding Kitchener in Cairo and levelled a pistol. Kitchener, in one of those strange interludes with personal danger, walked steadily towards the man with his hypnotic gaze fully trained on the young idealist, asking him what he wanted. The youth dropped the gun and fell on his knees, in which unfortunate position he was slashed to death by sabre-wielding guards who were not taking any chances. Some have argued that Kitchener would have done well to become British ambassador to Turkey in 1910, as his influence in the East was immense. It was believed that he might even have kept the Turks out of the war, thus avoiding the disaster at Gallipoli and freeing up Russian forces to concentrate on the Eastern Front against Germany. He was certainly a remarkable man with considerable personal charisma, and he understood the Oriental mind. A nationalist attack in India around this time severely wounded the Viceroy, Sir Charles Hardinge, and some years later the Sirdar of the Egyptian Army, Gen. Sir Lee Stack, was shot and killed by nationalists in 1924. British imperial posts were not without risk.

Whilst Churchill with his accustomed energy and boundless enthusiasm was familiarising himself with the workings of the Navy, visiting every port, naval station and ship he could reach in his official Admiralty yacht, the 4,000-ton *Enchantress* with a crew of 196, Lloyd George complained that Winston was becoming less and less interested in former political questions and more and more absorbed in boilers. 'You think we all live in the sea and all your thoughts are devoted to sea life, fishes and other aquatic creatures. You forget that most of us live on land.' In his *War Memoirs*, he commented: 'Mr Churchill's flammable fancy having caught fire with the idea of the monster ship, we had a battle over the naval estimates.'

Churchill had fallen under the influence of another remarkable man, Admiral Jackie Fisher, a restless, dynamic 73-year-old who fired out ideas like torpedoes in a never-ending stream of energy and excitement—just the sort of personality to captivate Churchill. The Navy did not have a General Staff like the War Office, its war plans being held in the heads of two admirals, Lord Fisher and Admiral Sir Arthur Wilson (nicknamed Old 'Ard Art'), another sailor of the old school, who was also in his seventies. These two were ready during any crisis to implement brisk naval actions that only they and the Foreign Secretary were privy to. Keeping most of the Cabinet in the dark about war plans was established government procedure and meant that apart from the Prime Minister, the Foreign Secretary and the heads of the Navy and Army, no one else was briefed or consulted. Fisher, flamboyant, mercurial and partial, succeeded in revolutionising the Navy, but at the same time divided it into conservative and radical camps. Admiral Charles Beresford was his main traditionalist enemy and the two fought a lasting feud. Wilson, as Second Sea Lord, was a taciturn, hard-working man who got on with the job. Fisher was forced to retire in 1910, partly as a result of this feud, but Churchill brought him back as First Sea Lord as soon as he could.

With two such powerful personalities demanding the need to upgrade the speed of ships by switching to oil propulsion instead of coal, the necessity of 15-inch (bore diameter) guns with greater ranges and increased displacements to keep them afloat (i.e. bigger ships) the £50 million naval estimates barrier was soon breached. Lloyd George as Chancellor at first opposed the increases, but eventually claimed to Churchill that he had been persuaded to a different point of view by his wife's homely questioning:

They say you are having an argument with that nice Mr Churchill about building Dreadnoughts. Of course I don't understand these things, but I should have thought it would be better to have too many rather than too few.

But there may have been another reason. In 1913, Lloyd George was embroiled in a scandal over the purchase of Marconi shares by certain members of the government, including himself, who knew of a lucrative contract offered to the British Marconi Company. Churchill and Asquith had stood by the embattled Chancellor when it appeared that his career might be jeopardised, and a board of inquiry at which Churchill gave evidence exonerated Lloyd George's somewhat dubious conduct. When Lloyd George finally caved in over the naval programme he might have had this instance of loyalty in mind, and the consideration that Churchill could prove an invaluable ally in the future. Churchill was in a sentimental mood (fuelled by alcohol) when he turned to Lloyd George at a dinner in John Morley's house in March 1914 and exclaimed: 'A wonderful thing our friendship! For ten years there has been hardly a day when we haven't had half an hour's talk together.' Another guest, Birrell, reportedly remarked, 'How awfully bored by this time you both must be.'

The assassination of an Austrian archduke on 28 June 1914 was soon pushed off the front pages by news of threatened civil war in Ulster and the sudden death of Joseph Chamberlain, who had been disabled by a stroke several years before, eliminating his powerful imperialist voice in the counsels of the realm. The Austrian ultimatum to Serbia a month later triggered several Cabinet discussions on the European situation. Asquith commented that it was the most dangerous situation of the last forty years, but did not expect Britain to be dragged into it.

Churchill was a consistent voice for intervention and supported Sir Edward Grey, who cited an old treaty guaranteeing the neutrality of Belgium, signed by Britain, France and Germany in 1839 and invoked by Gladstone in 1870 during the Franco-Prussian conflict. It had been designed primarily to limit the territorial ambitions of France as well as others, but was now to be used as a basis for any British intervention on its behalf. Kitchener, visiting London from Cairo, dined with the German ambassador, Prince Lichnowsky, and soon afterwards met with Asquith and Churchill, urging on Prime Minister Asquith the absolute necessity of standing by France. 'If we stood aside, our moral position would be such as to have lost us all respect.' Despite wobbles in Cabinet and a flurry of resignations and threats to resign over any warlike moves by Britain, Asquith achieved an agreement between the hawks and the doves that Britain would guarantee the neutrality of Belgium. Lloyd George, a member of the peace party, was able to reconcile his Liberal nonconformist conscience on this basis, although others, John Morley in particular, could not.

Meanwhile, vast continental military machines clattered into motion. Austrian artillery was already pounding the Serbian capital, Belgrade, when Czarist Russia ordered its enormous armies to mobilise in support of its Serbian cousins. The

Germans, supporting Austria-Hungary, did likewise, declaring war on Russia. France was asked to keep out of it, but keen to regain her territories of Alsace and Lorraine that had been lost in the Franco-Prussian conflict, and believing her armies a match for the Germans, particularly with powerful allies like Russia and Britain, replied that she would 'consult her interests'. At these fatal words the die was cast. Germany's infamous Schlieffen Plan swung into action and troop trains rumbled ominously towards the Belgian frontier. A dark shadow passed over the face of sunlit Europe and its shining summer seas. After decades of peace, the European empires at the height of their prosperity were to squander all in a disastrous war. The German plan relied entirely on a fast knockout blow delivered against France by an advance through neutral Belgium and the encirclement of Paris within forty days, so that the entire German Army could then turn to deal with Russia in support of its Austrian allies.

The British Cabinet had learned only two years previously that their military chiefs were far advanced in military and naval arrangements with French forces against such an event. 'Hostility scarcely represents the strength of the sentiment which the revelation aroused: it was more akin to consternation,' Lloyd George noted in his *War Memoirs*. Sir Edward Grey reassured the members that if war came, Britain would still be quite free to decide whether or not to participate. Gen. Sir Henry Wilson, who spent his summer holidays familiarising himself with the roads in Belgium he believed the Germans planned to use, had explained to the Cabinet with the aid of a big map and a pointer just what he expected to happen. Lloyd George and Churchill had then been very sceptical. Now the reality seemed very close.

Asquith told an emotional German ambassador, who implored him not to side with France, 'that we had no desire to intervene'. Germany could 'make intervention impossible' for Britain if it would respect the neutrality of Belgium and not attempt to use the Channel to attack the northern coasts of France. He authorised Grey to inform the French ambassador that the Royal Navy would oppose any attempt by the German fleet to enter the Channel for hostile operations. Andrew Bonar Law, on behalf of the Conservative and Unionist Party, sent word that they agreed that Britain must support France and Russia. Churchill had ordered the British fleet to remain together at the end of manoeuvres in the Channel on 28 July. He also bombarded Lloyd George with notes, pleading with him to bring 'your mighty aid to the discharge of our duty'.

The Kaiser, teetering on the brink of war with his English cousins (he was a grandson of Queen Victoria), even had second thoughts. He sent for his military chief, Von Moltke, and asked him if it would be possible to change the war plans and concentrate on Russia. The general replied that it was too late. All the preparations had been made on the assumption that the German Army would immediately march through Belgium and capture Paris in a given time. The Kaiser sent a special emissary to talk to Churchill, but any behind-the-scenes deal was rejected by the Cabinet.

Ordinary people throughout Europe clamoured for war. 'I shall never forget the warlike crowds that thronged Whitehall and poured into Downing Street while the

Cabinet deliberated on the alternatives of peace or war,' wrote Lloyd George. The crowd continued to grow and formed a dense mass from Trafalgar Square all the way to the House of Commons. Young men in taxi cabs passed along singing the 'Marseillaise' and waving Union Jacks. The roar of the crowds penetrated even to the Cabinet Room where portraits of former prime ministers stared impassively down, reminders of ancient struggles and accomplishments.

Foreign Secretary Grey made an eloquent speech to a packed House of Commons. Tuesday 4 August brought news that the German request to march through Belgium to attack France had been rejected by the Belgian king. The British government issued an ultimatum that unless Belgian neutrality was respected by Germany and assurances to that effect were received by twelve o'clock midnight (eleven o'clock British time), Britain would take steps to defend the treaty. Churchill was frantically busy with naval preparations at the Admiralty and fleets were on high alert across the globe.

Von Bethmann-Hollweg, the German Chancellor, is said to have responded, 'What—are England and Germany to go to war over a scrap of paper?' However, the ancient treaty was vital as a pretext to support France and unite the Cabinet. In his book *The World Crisis*, Churchill admitted that he had suspicions about Belgium's stance. 'All the great German preparations along the Belgian frontier, the intricate network of railways, the great camps' he thought suggested the existence of some secret agreement of free passage. 'I saw in Belgium a country with whom we had many differences over the Congo and other subjects.' But he was wrong. Very soon, German troops would be shooting civilians, even women and children, in their brutal march through the buffer state.

Kitchener, along with other heads of overseas missions, was heading back to his posting as Consul General in Cairo. He had taken the Calais boat train to Dover, where he impatiently paced the deck of his ship, demanding that it should get under way. While his aides argued with the captain, who was waiting for late passengers, a messenger appeared with an urgent summons from the Prime Minister. Kitchener was to return to London at once for an emergency meeting with leading members of the Cabinet. Ronald Storrs, his Egyptian Secretary, never forgot the look of dread on Kitchener's face as he read the message, or the feeling of resignation that accompanied them back to London. What Kitchener feared most was to be placed in some position immediately subordinate to a minister. He hated 'meddling' politicians and was used to glittering posts of autocratic control. But the Prime Minister had decided on a bold experiment—to place a soldier in charge of the War Office.

Asquith, after the ultimatum to Germany had been issued on his sole authority, without reference to the Cabinet, ruminated, 'Winston is longing for a sea fight in the early hours of tomorrow morning resulting in the sinking of the *Goeben* ... the whole thing fills me with sadness.' The *Goeben* a German battlecruiser, was being shadowed by Royal Navy ships in the Mediterranean. Roy Jenkins, Churchill's biographer, wrote that for Churchill the onset of war was a moment of exhilaration, the supreme contingency for which he had been preparing himself from his teenage days as a young subaltern seeking out the world's trouble spots. He was seen by one of Asquith's daughters striding towards the Cabinet Room, his face wreathed in smiles. In his letters to Clemmie, pregnant with their third child and safely ensconced in Norfolk, he deplored his tendencies to love the excitement of war, 'but I can't help it!'.

Lloyd George was more morose, like others in the Cabinet, and hoping that the last-minute threat of British involvement would arrest Germany's headlong rush to perdition:

> There were many of us who could hardly believe that those responsible for guiding the destiny of Germany would be so fatuous as deliberately to provoke the hostility of the British Empire with its inexhaustible reserves and with its grim tenacity of purpose once it engaged in a struggle.

Germany, aided by Austria-Hungary, was pitting itself against the armed strength of France, Russia and now Britain, all countries with long and illustrious military traditions. On the face of it, Germany was simply determined to commit suicide in a mad spectacle of national hubris, unless it recognised that the gamble of fighting just one or two of its chosen antagonists had failed. Surely it must draw back?

By the evening of 4 August no reply had been received from Berlin. Lloyd George joined Asquith, Grey and Haldane in the Cabinet Room soon after nine o'clock. A War Office censor had intercepted a telephone message from Berlin to the German ambassador in London, informing him that the British ambassador, Sir Edward Goschen, had at seven o'clock 'demanded his passport declaring war'. The Navy was prepared for sudden attack, but the ministers decided to wait until the midnight ultimatum expired in case the slightest possibility of peace remained.

> As the hour approached, a deep and tense solemnity fell on the room. No one spoke. [...] 'Boom!' the deep notes of Big Ben rang out into the night, the first strokes in Britain's most fateful hour. Every face was suddenly contracted in painful intensity. 'Doom, doom, doom,' to the last stroke.
>
> Twenty minutes after the hour Mr Winston Churchill came in and informed us that the wires had already been sent to the British ships of war in every sea announcing the fact that war had been declared and that they were to act accordingly. [...] We had challenged the most powerful military empire the world had yet brought forth.

Crowds cheered wildly as King George V was holding a Privy Council meeting for the issuing of proclamations. Lloyd George echoed the sentiments of another great British statesman, Sir Robert Walpole, who 175 years earlier when commenting on public joy at the outbreak of war, remarked, 'They are ringing their bells now, but soon they may be wringing their hands.'

# 7

# Total War

The concept of total or absolute war was formulated in a treatise by Prussian officer Carl Von Clausewitz, *On War*, published posthumously by his widow in 1832. He had served in the Prussian and Russian armies during the Napoleonic and French Revolutionary wars, and his book was an attempt to rationalise and systematically analyse the functions and possibilities of war and the reasons for conducting them.

He brought his experience of twenty years of European warfare and the study of 139 wars as the raw material for his task. His underlying purpose was to reconcile theory and practice; the justification or condemnation of war he left to others. According to Von Clausewitz, the practical purpose of war was 'the continuation of state policy by other means'. He foresaw a time when entire populations would be involved in the process of war, so that everyone was affected, instead of wars being conducted by professionals at one remove while normal life continued for everyone else. However, he believed in the primacy of the political process in deciding the onset, practicable duration and objective of all wars. During warfare overall political control should never pass to the military chiefs, but they should be strictly allowed to get on with the exercise of their professional calling without undue interference from government in operational questions. They could advise politicians on the problems and plans of operation and on overall strategy, but the ultimate responsibility for beginning and ending wars rested with politicians.

The closest equivalent of modern war in Europe had been the Franco-Prussian war of 1870. Trains had been used to move troops to the Front; telegraphy and aerial observation balloons had been used to direct artillery fire; modern breech loading weapons with greater range and accuracy had changed battlefield tactics. Apart from some protracted sieges, it had been a comparatively fast-moving war and the French Army had been strategically overwhelmed by the Prussian war plan.

When the British War Council convened after Britain had declared war on Germany, most of the military chiefs had this previous war in mind and their already existing plans of co-ordination with Belgian and French allies, to counter the expected moves of the German steamroller. They were thinking in terms of a European war, and a pretty fast-moving one at that. After all, Napoleon had been smashed by one battle at Waterloo just a century before. Only one man thought otherwise, and said so repeatedly. Lord Kitchener had been asked by Asquith to attend the first meetings as an adviser and he listened to the suggestions and objections thrown up by the other senior generals present. Lord Roberts wanted to know if the Army might concentrate around Antwerp, the major Belgian port. The plan to concentrate alongside the French at Maubeuge was criticised by several officers as too far forward, and they suggested Amiens, or a landing and concentration at Antwerp to co-operate with the Belgian and Dutch armies. This would force the Germans to slow their attack in order to deal with a powerful threat on their right as they pushed into France. It had the potential drawback of dividing the British from their French allies and, as co-operation with the powerful French Army was paramount, it was ignored. Gen. Sir Henry Wilson, an impetuous Irishman who had drawn up the mobilisation plans, was impatient of Kitchener's caution. 'They discussed strategy like idiots,' he sneered.

The immediate result of this first meeting was the appointment the following day, 6 August, of Kitchener as Secretary for War. The post had been held by the Prime Minister, and although Haldane was willing to take it up again and was in fact the architect of the war plan along with Sir Henry Wilson, Director of Military Operations, Asquith felt the role would be better served for political as well as military reasons by Kitchener at the War Office. Lloyd George later explained:

> His selection for what was practically a War Dictatorship gave satisfaction and confidence to the nation generally and to the Conservative Party in particular. It undoubtedly had the effect of restraining criticism, for doubts cast on the War direction implied censure of Lord Kitchener. For the first few months of the War his influence was paramount. His very picture on the walls counted more than all the appeals of all the political leaders of all parties.

Determined to stand staunchly beside his French allies, Kitchener dispatched the British Expeditionary Force (BEF) of four out of six infantry divisions and one cavalry division amounting to 100,000 highly trained regular soldiers, many already battle-seasoned from the South African campaigns, to the forward rendezvous in France. He was sceptical of French commander Marshal Joffre's conviction that the Germans would fall in with his carefully laid battle plans and march directly on France by the nearest route. Kitchener was convinced that the Germans would march along all eleven roads in Belgium that crossed the frontier and attempt to outflank the Allies further to the north. This is exactly what happened at Mons, when overwhelming German forces attacked the British, proving Kitchener's instinct right and Wilson's wrong.

Kitchener faced two primary tasks once mobilisation was under way: finding enough men to build up an army of sufficient force, and finding enough ammunition to keep the guns firing. On 6 August, the government authorised an increase to the Army of half a million men, and the first recruiting posters appeared in the streets the following day. Kitchener was aiming to recruit at least 100,000 men immediately for the regular army. Recruitment stands were set up everywhere and men flocked to join, impelled by posters showing Kitchener's bristling moustache and pointing finger, with the stirring admonition 'Your Country Needs You!' Before the year was out, not 100,000 but 1,180,000 men had volunteered, with 35,000 joining up in one day during August! In no war before or since has this phenomenon of beaming men flocking in their thousands to recruiting stations and queuing for hours in euphoric good humour for the privilege of receiving a little chit of paper telling them that they had been accepted to leave their bones in France, Belgium or the Levant, as it turned out for so many.

The new minister's maiden speech in the House of Lords outlined Britain's needs:

> The Empires with whom we are at war have called to the colours almost their entire male population. The principle which we shall observe is that while their maximum forces steadily diminish, our reinforcements shall steadily flow out, until we have an army in the field in numbers and quality not unworthy of the power and responsibilities of the British Empire.

Days before, Kitchener told the Cabinet to prepare for a war that would last at least three years and certainly would not be over by Christmas, as some optimists imagined. It would require a vaster army than Britain had ever fielded before. Time would be needed, and the earliest the Kitchener Volunteers could be trained, armed, and ready for France, was spring 1915. Britain had sent just five divisions to France in the BEF, two divisions having been retained for home defence. Other regular troops were being shipped in from the garrisons of the Empire. What was proposed was nothing less than the creation of seventy more divisions out of nothing!

By mid-August the Royal Navy had the tricky job of ferrying the bulk of the Army across the Channel, mindful of sudden attack by the German fleet. Sea lanes were mined, the British Grand Fleet cruised south from its position off northern Scotland, and the French fleet covered the southern approaches. This was the time when Germany might have made a mad dash across the North Sea to land 20,000 men on the east coast of England as a distraction in order to divert the energies of the British from aiding the French. However, they missed the opportunity and were so badly informed that until the first clash between British and German cavalry occurred, they did not even know that most of the BEF was already in France. This was a quiet success that might have been a total disaster. It had been achieved thanks to Churchill's preparation immediately after fleet manoeuvres in the Channel at the end of July, and the rounding-up of 120 German spies in Britain by the police and MI5. The Kaiser raged at his intelligence staff for a full two hours. 'Am I surrounded by dolts?' he cried.

Churchill wrote:

Imagine this great Fleet with its flotillas and cruisers steaming slowly out of Portland harbour, squadron by squadron, scores of gigantic castles of steel wending their way across the misty, shining sea, like giants bowed in anxious thought [...] as darkness fell, eighteen miles of warships running at high speed and in absolute blackness [lights extinguished] through the narrow straights. We looked at each other with considerable satisfaction when the Flagship reported herself and the whole Fleet well out in the centre of the North Sea.

Thus, even before war was declared, the Navy had achieved a *coup de main* and placed itself in a blocking position to frustrate any move by the German High Seas Fleet.

Churchill was busy day and night interpreting his role as 'ruler of the King's Navee' (to paraphrase Gilbert and Sullivan) in what was to become a typically Churchillian fashion. Clausewitz's 'primacy of politics' was certainly not breached in his case. Operational responsibility was supposed to belong to the First Sea Lord, Admiral Prince Louis of Battenberg, in consultation with Churchill as the First Lord of the Admiralty. In fact, it operated the other way round. Churchill was issuing a stream of operational orders, which were stamped 'I concur' by the hapless Battenberg, who felt his position compromised by the anti-German prejudice then growing in the service (as he was cousin to the Kaiser). His days, of course, were numbered. Churchill soon brought his favourite, Admiral Jackie Fisher, out of retirement to fill the role. But whereas Battenberg easily gave way to Churchill's overbearing rhetoric, Fisher was to become more of a stumbling block. Their partnership at first, however, went through a honeymoon period.

Churchill described his commanding role at the Admiralty thus:

I accepted full responsibility for bringing about successful results, and in that spirit I exercised a close general supervision over everything that was done or proposed. Further I claimed and exercised an unlimited power of suggestion and initiative over the whole field, subject only to the approval and agreement of the First Sea Lord on all operative orders.

His first experience, early in August, was a chastising one. The German battlecruiser *Goeben*, accompanied by the smaller cruiser *Breslau*, managed to slip past Royal Navy squadrons charged with protecting French troop transports across the Mediterranean. Despite a flurry of precise instructions to intercept them, signalled to admirals on the spot by Churchill, after refuelling at Messina in neutral Italy the German ships had unexpectedly steamed for Constantinople where the *Goeben* and the *Breslau* were 'sold' to the Turks, effectively bringing the Ottoman Empire into the war on the side of Germany, bristling as the country was over the many slights it had endured at the hands of Britain and France over Egypt and many other issues.

Otherwise, British sea power ruled unchallenged. Except in the Baltic Sea, where Germany maintained vital trade with Sweden and other Baltic countries, the German merchant fleet remained bottled up in neutral ports, and German battleships in far foreign seas hid themselves in the illimitable ocean vastness. The swarming merchant fleet of Britain after a brief hesitation, and backed by government insurance, soon continued to trade as prolifically as before. British submarines and destroyers blockaded the Heligoland Bight, making any attempt by the German High Seas Fleet to enter the North Sea a most hazardous enterprise. But they had some aces up their sleeves and would soon play them.

Freed from his indecision once war was declared, Lloyd George now threw himself into dealing with the immediate monetary crisis. As Chancellor of the Exchequer he acted with the Governor of the Bank of England to quell fears among city financiers. London was the finance capital of the world and a bank moratorium had been declared, which lasted until 10 August, effectively suspending business. Lloyd George later recalled:

> There are those who pretend to believe that this was a war intrigued and organised by financiers for their own purpose. I was Chancellor and saw money before the war; I saw it immediately after the outbreak of war; I lived with it for days, and did my best to steady its nerve, for I knew how much depended on its confidence; and I say that money was a frightened and trembling thing; money shivered at the prospect. It is a foolish and ignorant thing to call this a financiers' war.

He welcomed the party truce that suspended discussion of such controversial issues as Irish Home Rule and Welsh disestablishment for the duration, and his handling of the financial crisis impressed even the critical economist Keynes.

However, Lloyd George's attention also wandered to the inefficiency he detected in other departments of government. Having taken over at the War Office, Kitchener was struggling with red tape, and Lloyd George commented:

> Unhappily the War Office was hampered by a traditional reactionism. Its policy seemed to be that of preparing not for the next war, but for the last one, or the last but one. The Boer War found us in the mentality of the Crimea [fought in the 1850s] and the Great War caught our military thinkers planning for the next war under the conditions of the Alma [a Crimean battle] in so far as these were modified by the irrelevant experiences of the African veldt. Unfortunately they only remembered the lessons that were better forgotten because they were inapplicable, and forgot all the experiences by which they ought to have profited because they were a foretaste of the methods of future warfare [...] Military imagination makes up in retentiveness what it misses in agility.

While Kitchener was doing his best to sort out this mess and gear up the hidebound War Office for a major European conflict, the Schlieffen Plan had flung seven-eighths of the German Army at France, outnumbering the British and French armies combined. Fortunately, Von Moltke, the new commander-in-chief, was tempted to modify his dead uncle's original plan. He kept 20 per cent in reserve and then moved troops from France to counter the attack of the Russians in East Prussia. This was just enough to tip the balance in favour of the Allies. Applied at four-fifths of its intensity, the great right-wheeling thrust only nearly succeeded. It was a close-run thing. This is how it happened. Churchill recorded:

> Late on the evening of August 23rd I had a talk with Lord Kitchener. We knew that the main battle had been joined and that our men had been fighting all day; but he had received no news. He was darkly hopeful.

Kitchener indicated on the map that a vigorous French counter-stroke from Namur might well cut the German Army and trap its forward divisions between the French and the British. Churchill continued:

> At 7 o'clock next morning, I was sitting up in bed in Admiralty House working at my boxes, when the door of my bedroom opened and Lord Kitchener appeared. He had a bowler hat on his head which he took off and a slip of paper in his hand. He paused in the doorway and I knew in a flash that the event had gone wrong. Though his manner was quite calm, his face was different. I had the subconscious feeling that it was distorted and discoloured, as if he had been punched with a fist. His eyes rolled more than ever. His voice too was hoarse. He looked gigantic. 'Bad news,' he said heavily and laid the slip of paper on my bed.

It was a telegram from Sir John French, commanding the BEF:

> My troops have been engaged all day with the enemy on a line roughly east and west through Mons. The attack was renewed after dark, but we held our ground tenaciously. I have just received a message from the General commanding the French 5th Army that his troops have been driven back, that Namur has fallen, and that he is taking up a line from Maubeuge to Rocroi. I have therefore ordered a retirement [...] It will prove a difficult operation if the enemy remains in contact.

Churchill and Kitchener were shocked at the strategic implications. A strong fortress at Namur garrisoned by French and Belgian troops had fallen in just one day! The German thrust was not going to be arrested by a French counter-stroke. Would it sweep on to the Channel ports, cutting the BEF off from its naval lifeline? In fact, the Germans had encountered a setback they had not bargained for, and a considerable blow to their morale—(for them) the previously unsuspected military prowess of the British Army!

But this was not known immediately to the ministers in London. Churchill hurried across to consult with Lloyd George, who recalled his worried face as he beckoned him across the room from a busy meeting. Churchill said later:

With this fateful news I felt intensely the need of contact with him. I wanted to know how it would strike him and how he would face it. I made my way to the Treasury Boardroom. As I opened the door I saw that it was crowded. One of that endless series of conferences with all the great business and financial authorities of Britain, by means of which the corner was turned, was in progress. He saw me at once: I beckoned with my finger and he came out. We went into a little room scarcely bigger than a cupboard and I told him what had happened. I was relieved and overjoyed at his response. He was once again the Lloyd George of Agadir. Not since that morning of the Mansion House speech, three years before, had I seen him so strong and resolute for our country or so sure of its might.

It was the indomitable spirit of these two men that fixed the pivot on which the whole war machine of Britain would swing.

Sir John French's little army had done well. Von Kluck's 1st Army attacking it was the strongest in the German invasion force. The numbers engaged on each side were comparable with those of the British versus the French at Waterloo, fought not far from Mons a century before. Like the Duke of Wellington's men, in facing superior odds the British had made defensive positions alongside suitable features—in this case the Mons–Condé Canal. The Germans had come on in massed columns in the same old way as Napoleon's men, the British infantry firing from almost invisible positions driving them back in the same old way. Churchill was convinced that the lack of recent experience would lead the Germans to underestimate the firepower and devastating range of modern weapons. And so it proved. Two canal bridges with machine guns mounted on them held back the German advance for a considerable time, together with the unbelievable rate of accurate fire by British riflemen and field artillery.

German units had been surprised by the sudden appearance of British bicycle troops on 21 August, when Pte John Parr became the first British casualty of the Great War. Early next day, the 4th Dragoon Guards ambushed and chased German cavalry units, Capt. Hornby killing or wounding a German Lancer with his sabre and riding back to display his bloody blade. Von Kluck was positively ordered not to try to outflank the British too far north in case he became separated from the main German thrust. His decision to make a frontal attack cost him dear. After their first heavy casualties, the Germans advanced against the unseen enemy in loose open order and reached the canal. Lt Maurice Dease of the Royal Fusiliers was soon operating the Vickers machine gun on Nimy Bridge by himself, the entire gun crew having been picked off. He continued firing until he had been hit five times, finally dying of his wounds. At Ghlin Bridge, Pte Sidney Godley defied the hail of fire as the only remaining machine gunner and held back the attackers all day, even covering the withdrawal of the Fusiliers on the canal bank in the evening and then dismantling the gun and throwing it into the canal. Both men were awarded VCs, the first of the war.

Sir John French was now told by Gen. Charles Lanrezac of the French 5th Army that he was withdrawing in the face of heavy German attacks and advised him to do the same. Sir John, who would not have looked out of place at a farmer's mart with his heavy features and straggling white moustache, had a similar regard for his men as a farmer might for prize beef cattle. He was willing to part with some of them, but only at a high price, and he positively intended to keep others for breeding future strains of a winning stock. (He needed officers and sergeants to train new soldiers.) After falling back to a prepared second line the order was given to continue the retreat. The British Tommies were nonplussed. Had they not given the Huns a bloody nose?

The German soldiers themselves were in no doubt of this. Hauptmann (Capt.) Walter Bloem wrote, 'We are exhausted and chilled to the bone and have suffered a heavy, heavy defeat. There is no denying it—and at the hands of the despised English, whom we laughed at only hours before.' There were up to 8,000 German casualties and fewer than 2,000 British. The German steamroller had temporarily halted, with their buglers blowing the ceasefire. Had Lanrezac's troops been able to come to reinforce Sir John French's well-held position, just like the Prussians had come to the aid of Wellington at Waterloo, things might have been different. But that would have opened a gap in the French line, and Lanrezac was moving away rapidly south. The BEF was obliged to follow.

The retreat went on for days. More guns were lost than at any time since the Crimea. Finally, the footsore Tommies of II Corps were halted by Smith-Dorrien, one of French's subordinate generals, and fought a tenacious rearguard action at Le Cateau, halting the Germans but at tremendous cost—nearly 8,000 British casualties, or as many as the enemy had lost at Mons. Sir John French was furious. He now believed that the troops should withdraw to the Channel port of Le Havre, and telegraphed to London for permission, as in any event, he had lost contact with Lanrezac's 5th Army.

Whether or not Kitchener saw this as his moment to take supreme command (he said he would have liked Cromwell's title of Captain General) is unclear, but he immediately told the Cabinet he was going to put some iron into Sir John French's soul, and ordered the troubled general to a meeting in Paris. When they met at the British Embassy in Paris, Kitchener, wearing his field marshal's uniform, was described as looking calm and reflective, while Sir John was irritable and surly, telling everyone that the meeting must be short as he was desperately needed at the Front. Kitchener took him into a private room and what passed between them is unrecorded. But it was probably an ultimatum along the lines of 'Do as I say, or else I'll find someone who will.' When they came out, Kitchener had an agreement from the commander-in-chief that his army would continue to co-operate with the French under Joffre. A telegram was sent to London: 'He will remain conforming to the movements of the French Army, though at the same time acting with caution to avoid being unsupported on his flanks.' Sir John affected to be satisfied with this, but privately complained that Kitchener had no business wearing his field marshal's uniform and pulling rank when he was supposed to be a minister!

Churchill had written an encouraging note to Sir John and received a grateful reply. 'It was a keen pleasure to hear from you ... Our troops have suffered severely, but they are simply glorious! I can't find words to say all I think of them.' By 10 September, the French and British had massively counter-attacked and were pursuing the Germans. The 'Miracle of the Marne' had occurred, when the entire British Army marched into a gap spotted between two German armies by Allied aircraft, and a battle lasting several days and involving two-and-a-half million men became a turning point. The French brought up a critical reinforcement of 6,000 reservists from Paris in a fleet of Renault taxicabs, and the Germans were flung back with up to 220,000 casualties. Retreating rapidly, survivors dug in on a defensive line near the River Aisne, establishing the first permanent trench systems of the war. Von Moltke suffered a nervous collapse, reporting to the Kaiser, 'Your Majesty, we have lost the war.' A dash by the British to secure the Channel ports and the coast near the Belgian port of Antwerp ensued. At the British GHQ, Gen. Sir Henry Wilson, now sub-chief of staff to Sir John French, marched up and down clapping his hands together and repeating, 'To the sea, to the sea, we shall never get to the sea!'

At this critical moment Churchill was sent to Antwerp to stiffen the Belgian government's resolve in holding the port against the Germans. Striding about in a cape and a yachting cap and smoking innumerable cigars amid the howl of incoming shells, he rehearsed his later role in the Second World War. He had brought along the Naval Division and an armoured car brigade (consisting of commandeered Rolls-Royces hastily fitted with armour plating) for the defence of the city. Kitchener sent what soldiers he could spare, energetically supporting his young colleague, and was even prepared to appoint Churchill a temporary lieutenant general and military governor, recognising his fighting spirit. But Churchill's offer to resign as First Lord to become a general was 'greeted with a Homeric laugh' by his Cabinet colleagues, according to Asquith, who liked Greek tragedies. 'Winston is an ex-lieutenant of Hussars, and would (if the offer were accepted) be in command of several distinguished major generals, brigadiers and colonels!' He had no intention of losing him from the Admiralty. At least not for the time being.

In fact, Churchill spent more time in France and Belgium than any of his Cabinet colleagues. He set up a Naval Air Squadron at Dunkirk, which harassed the enemy and attacked Zeppelins on the ground in Germany, and commandeered London omnibuses to ferry around Marines and Territorial battalions, who were hastily improvised for the defence of the Channel ports. He personally directed military operations around Antwerp with the help of the commander of Marines, General Paris, flitting from watching street fighting amid the clatter of machine guns in the suburbs to the tranquillity of downtown Antwerp. 'Twenty minutes in a motorcar and we were back in the warmth and light of one of the best hotels in Europe, with its perfectly appointed tables and attentive servants all proceeding as usual!' His biographer Jenkins believed that Churchill insisted on luxury as his due, alongside his undoubted ability to rough it and take risks that others would avoid.

The defence of Antwerp for five days and the flooding of the dikes slowed the enemy sufficiently for the Channel ports to be secured by Sir John French moving his army from the Aisne to face the Germans at Ypres. The Royal Navy was bombarding the German Army's advance along the coast at Ostend with anything that could be flung at them. Ironclad monitors, gunboats, destroyers, cruisers and even some old and expendable battleships could be brought near enough, at high tide, to pound the enemy and secure the left flank of the British line. 'We scoured the dockyards for every little vessel that carried a gun of any kind ... even gunboats 40 years old were pressed into service and, one way or another, fire was constantly maintained.'

In late August a daring raid by several Royal Navy squadrons on flotillas around Heligoland—an island fortress and forward German naval base in the North Sea— had resulted in the sinking of three German cruisers, one of their destroyers and the capture of 335 prisoners, including a son of Von Tirpitz, head of the German Navy. This had so shaken the Kaiser that he gave the bottling order: no major naval raid or movement of their fleet without his express authority. So apart from German submarines and torpedo boats, the naval operations in the Channel went unhindered. This was as well, for the Royal Navy soon faced less auspicious news and Churchill, already criticised for his swaggering role at Antwerp, was eagerly blamed by his detractors both inside and outside the Cabinet for any failure.

Kitchener, meanwhile, was under mounting pressure to send Sir John French the two things in short supply—munitions and men. Up to 58,000 officers and men of the BEF had become casualties, or were rendered out of action, and the momentous battle for Ypres was making fresh inroads on the army. But the War Minister was determined to do two things: hold some regular army divisions back, to counter any German attack on the homeland; and resist calls for his barely trained volunteers to be sent immediately to the Front. This last was common sense, as many men who answered his call had no uniforms, were drilling with broomsticks, and camping in church halls and playing fields. Reserve list NCOs, who last fought in the South African War, were called up to drill and train them, while retired captains and majors were summoned to lead battalions as colonels and brigadiers. Asquith commented with wry humour that it was a sight to see 'Winston drooling at all these glittering commands going to "dugouts"'. In fact, Churchill's dynamism mystified his more indolent colleagues.

'Churchill is like a torpedo,' commented his friend Lloyd George. 'The first you know he is up to something is the swish of him rushing by.' Few of them had any idea of just how much he was 'up to'. His detailed list of activities is meticulously recorded in *The World Crisis* and Admiralty minutes, and far from the Navy having little to do in the opening months of the war, its operations were vital in every theatre. The Naval Air Squadrons were providing the only aerial home defence over ports, fuel dumps, towns and cities, as well as attacking the enemy air force on its own territory. The armoured car had been developed on Churchill's authority to protect the forward air bases in France and led on to the development of the tracked and armoured tank. The Navy had neutralised the German High Seas Fleet, was chasing their remaining cruisers at sea, combating submarines and torpedo boats, and guarding troop and supply convoys. In addition, it was now to support operations to seize German overseas territories.

Lloyd George had been busy with war finance, but now he stepped into the limelight with a patriotic and stirring speech at the Queen's Hall in late September. After criticising Germany's violation of Belgium and its likening of treaties to 'scraps of paper', he averred that national honour and that of the British Empire was at stake in a matter of supreme principle. 'They think we cannot beat them. It will not be easy. It will be a long job; it will be a terrible war; but in the end we shall march through terror to triumph.' Then, in an imaginative foray back to his boyhood, he described a beautiful valley he had known, sheltered from the bitter blasts of the wind, snug and comfortable but very enervating:

> We have been too comfortable and too indulgent, many, perhaps, too selfish, and the stern hand of fate has scourged us to an elevation where we can see the everlasting things that matter for a nation—the great peaks we had forgotten, of Honour, Duty, Patriotism, and clad in glittering white, the towering pinnacle of Sacrifice pointing like a rugged finger to Heaven.

The response on the night was mixed and Lloyd George felt that the speech had been unsuccessful, but the press and politicians loved it. It was reprinted and widely circulated, but Celtic imagination does not always go down too well with a phlegmatic Anglo-Saxon audience. Perhaps they were expecting facts and figures from their Chancellor, mingled with some practical reassurance, instead of an uplifting sermon sprinkled with colourful metaphors. As also the colour of sacrifice is generally red, it may have been noted in some quarters that Lloyd George was doing his best to ensure that his own sons got comparatively safe jobs as staff officers, although they did see action later in the war.

Round about this time the Royal Navy, about which Britons had always been inordinately proud, suffered a series of heavy blows. A single German submarine managed to get between and sink three elderly armoured cruisers on a regular patrol off the Dutch coast—two of them while they were trying to pick up survivors from the first ship—and 1,400 men were lost. Even worse, a highly expensive modern Dreadnought, the *Audacious*, hit a mine or was torpedoed off the coast of Northern Ireland. Half a week later, Admiral Cradock and 1,600 sailors of the cruisers *Monmouth* and *Good Hope* perished in the cruel seas off Chile in the Battle of Coronel. The British ships, silhouetted against the sunset, were easy targets for the flotilla under Admiral Von Spee, almost invisible with his back to the darkened Chilean coast. Hunted across the globe by vengeful warships, Von Spee met his own destiny a month later at the Battle of the Falklands. As the *Gneisenau*, the leading armoured cruiser, approached the Falklands' main harbour intending to attack the coaling station, a pair of tripod masts sharply visible in the clear morning air were seen behind the promontory, indicating the presence of a Dreadnought. 'They meant certain death,' wrote Churchill. 'There was no hope of victory. There was no chance of escape.'

As the German cruiser and its escort turned back towards the *Scharnhorst* and the main flotilla, Admiral Sturdee's squadron steamed out of the harbour in pursuit, confident that their steady 20 knots would soon overtake the German ships which managed only 18 knots. At 16,000 yards range, the British guns opened fire on the light cruisers lagging behind the bigger ships. Von Spee turned to face his antagonists, hoping to close the range so that his guns could come into play. But first the *Scharnhorst* and then the *Gneisenau* were pounded into wrecks by the British 12-inch guns, both sinking. Only 200 survivors were pulled from the icy waters, most of whom died of shock from the cold. The remaining German light cruisers were hunted down and sunk one by one. As the *Nürnberg* sank, a group of defiant sailors could be seen on the stern waving to the last the German flag.

On 3 November 1914, the bizarre event of German armoured cruisers bombarding Great Yarmouth on the Norfolk coast occurred. 'What did it mean?' demanded Churchill. 'Obviously it was intended as a demonstration to divert the British fleet from something else.' An intervention on the Belgian coast, a foray into the Channel or a descent on the British Isles were all possibilities. Instead they steamed away and nothing followed.

Kitchener and planners at the War Office were all convinced that an invasion of Britain was now a real possibility. He had kept back two regular divisions and another of volunteers was deemed sufficiently trained for home defence. Admiral Fisher had just taken over as First Sea Lord at the Admiralty on the resignation of Battenberg and threw himself into changing the dispositions of naval forces around Britain's shores. The War Office and Admiralty estimated that the Germans could easily spare a quarter of a million first-rate troops for an attempted landing. Churchill was sceptical at first but, 'I allowed myself to succumb to the suppressed excitement which grew throughout the highest circles and did my utmost to speed our preparations'.

The 2nd Fleet was brought to the Thames, and the 3rd Battle Squadron was detached from the Grand Fleet at Scapa Flow, despite the objections of the commander-in-chief Sir John Jellicoe, and sailed south to the Firth of Forth. Battleships were redistributed along east coast ports, mines were laid, patrols were stepped up. But the crisis passed with the favourable moon and tides, and Fisher urged Churchill to encourage Kitchener to send 100,000 regulars to Flanders to reinforce the BEF. A request was also received from Joffre, asking for naval bombardment against German forces between Ostend and Nieuport on the Belgian coast to be stepped up. Old battleships, including the *Revenge*, were sent to do this dangerous inshore work, and a new class of boat developed by Churchill and Fisher in larger numbers, the shallow-draught, armoured, turtle-backed monitors, began to prove useful. Fitted with anti-mine and torpedo 'crinolines', they were low in the water, making difficult targets for both ship and shore batteries, and were fitted with very heavy guns up to 15 inches in diameter.

> On the morning of December 16th at about half past eight I was in my bath, when the door opened and an officer came hurrying in from the War Room with a naval signal which I grasped with a dripping hand. 'German battlecruisers bombarding Hartlepool.' I jumped out of the bath with exclamations [...] Pulling on clothes over a damp body I ran downstairs to the War Room.

Churchill recalled officers were darting about and the room was a hive of activity. Chief of staff Admiral Oliver was marking positions on the map, and signals were pouring in from naval stations along the coast and intercepts from British ships in the vicinity. The 2nd Battle Squadron of cruisers and powerful battleships patrolling 150 miles to the east seemed guaranteed to cut off the retreat of the German cruisers. Other squadrons and the Grand Fleet were called out, and submarines around the Heligoland Bight were put on alert for the return of the raiders.

The home defence forces at Hartlepool had attempted to return fire with field guns. Their reward was to receive salvoes that destroyed rows of adjoining terraced streets. Similar destruction ensued at Whitby, then Scarborough, fortunately denuded of visitors, as the German ships steamed along the coast before heading into the increasing haze and disappearing in fog banks. By lunchtime the Navy had discovered that the German High Seas Fleet had also slipped out from Cuxhaven. A powerful British squadron was now steaming towards possible destruction at their hands, locked between them and the raiders. Such an encounter might seriously alter the balance of naval power were the British force to be destroyed before the Grand Fleet could arrive.

Churchill's confident reports to the War Committee of the Cabinet earlier in the day now lost much of their swagger. Von Tirpitz later wrote, 'Admiral Von Ingenohl had the fate of Germany in the palm of his hand. I boil with emotion whenever I think of it.' But the German admiral felt hampered by the Kaiser's 'muzzling order'. On seeing the gun flashes of British destroyers engaging his cruiser screen, he turned tail, believing he would be attacked with torpedoes in darkness, risking his capital ships. By 6 p.m. the two main naval forces were only fifty miles apart; by 8 p.m. Admiral Wilson in the War Room said, 'Well, there you are, they have got away.' Only one British submarine found itself near enough to the German squadrons as they steamed home through the Heligoland Bight. It released two torpedoes in the rough seas, but they missed their targets and the ships passed unmolested.

The British press were quick to censure 'naval incompetence'. What was the Admiralty doing? Were they all asleep? How had this happened? There were 500 British civilians killed or wounded, and the outrage had neither been prevented nor avenged by the most powerful navy in the world! Churchill came in for much of the blame:

> We had to bear in silence the censures of our countrymen. We could never admit for fear of compromising our secret information where our squadrons were, or how near the German raiding cruisers had been to their destruction.

Likewise the British public would never realise how closely the destruction of a large British naval force had been avoided.

Asquith's comment on Churchill, 'He is so resourceful and undismayed: two of the qualities I like best,' were not always reflected in the First Lord's own secret feelings. Churchill later wrote:

> I do not remember any period when the weight of the war seemed to press more heavily on me than these months. In spite of being accustomed to years of abuse, I could not but feel the adverse and hostile currents that flowed about me.

At least he had called to his side a man hailed as 'the most distinguished naval officer since Nelson'. Lord Fisher was back at the helm of the Admiralty as First Sea Lord. In his previous tenure up to 1911, he had utterly modernised the Navy, scrapping outdated ships and ordering modern replacements. 'His genius was deep and true. Above all he was in harmony with the vast size of events. Like them he was built on a titanic scale,' Churchill wrote of the man he admired and worked well with—certainly in the beginning.

Fisher was almost 74 years old; his deputy, Sir Arthur Wilson, was not much younger, but these two had more sea miles, knowledge and stature than any other officers of the Navy. To lessen the burden on an old man, Churchill did turn about with him. The admiral retired to rest at about 8 p.m., awaking refreshed at 4 or 5 a.m. to begin his working day. By afternoon his powers were declining, and early evening found him exhausted by the hourly demands on his concentration. 'Still, judged from the point of view of physical and mental vigour alone, it was a wonderful effort and one which filled me, who watched him closely, with admiration and, I will add, reassurance,' wrote Churchill, who altered his day to fit in with Fisher's hours, starting later in the morning and finishing in the small hours. 'I had not previously seen the pulse of the Admiralty beat so strong and regular.'

As Christmas 1914 came and went without a conclusion, other than a brief and spontaneous truce among the soldiers that saw the British and Germans playing football in no man's land between the trenches (until suppressed by the higher command), both Lloyd George and Churchill submitted strategies of their own for breaking the deadlock. One was favoured by Kitchener, the other by Fisher. Prime Minister Asquith, lofty and detached, like an Oxford don or the judge he might have been, prevaricated for a second and third opinion. 'Have you ever heard him express an idea of his own?' a colleague remarked. No one had.

# 8

# A Soft Underbelly

*They will think they have seen the sun at night,*
*When they will see the pig half-man:*
*Noise, song, battle, fighting in the sky perceived,*
*And one will hear brute beasts talking.*
Prophesies of Michel de Nostredame (Nostradamus), 1555

The year 1915 began with a search for an alternative to the stalemate on the Western Front—several schemes being submitted to the Prime Minister. Asquith remarked that he had received two long memos, 'one from Winston, the other from Lloyd George (quite good the latter)!' and another from the Cabinet Secretary, Col. Maurice Hankey.

Churchill was currently keen on capturing the German island of Borkum, off the mouth of the River Ems and a few miles north of the Dutch coast, as a preliminary to landing an army in Schleswig-Holstein threatening the Kiel Canal and naval penetration of the Baltic, having drawn Denmark into the war. This had been a favoured plan of Fisher and Arthur Balfour, the former Conservative leader who was now very friendly with Winston and spending time with him at the Admiralty. But Fisher was rather cool about it and spoke airily of forcing an entry into the Baltic to threaten German trade without explaining how it might be tactically possible. It seems highly likely that he simply wished to play a waiting game until the German fleet came out for the decisive battle. Churchill and Fisher were already getting on one another's nerves, as both wanted their own way. At the beginning of January, Fisher offered his resignation when his advice to Churchill, that a German civilian hostage should be shot for every civilian killed by Zeppelin raids on Britain, was turned down. Churchill told the admiral:

> The question of aerial defence is not one upon which you have any professional experience. The question of killing prisoners in reprisal for an aerial attack is not one for the Admiralty, and certainly not for you to decide [...] After much reflection I cannot support it.

Churchill had ordered the building of aircraft for the Navy, but remained sceptical of the usefulness of airships. 'I could not help but feel that the inflammable gas made them easy targets and very vulnerable,' he wrote.

Lloyd George was convinced that continued offensives against German defences in the West would merely result in 'appalling loss of life' and achieve nothing. His idea was for a stab at the soft underbelly of the Austrian and Ottoman empires by attacking via Salonika on the Adriatic coast, with the help of Greece and Serbia, and landing troops in Syria, 'thus knocking Germany's props from under her'. He was also very concerned about the munitions problem. 'You remember the guns and ammunition incident? When I raised the question in Cabinet the War Office had only ordered 600 guns in all—those were to be delivered by next September!'

After the Allied victory at Ypres in November and stabilisation of the Front, Sir John French had been looking towards an advance northwards along the Belgian coast supported by the Navy, which was concerned at the use of Zeebrugge as a German submarine base. However, Marshal Joffre vetoed this for political as well as military reasons and insisted on a French Division being posted on the Allied line between the British and Belgian armies. Instead, more troops were earmarked to be squandered on frontal assaults.

The plan that came to be favoured by all, after Cabinet discussion, was that proposed initially by Hankey. On the face of it, it was a very clever strategy to knock Turkey out of the war by cutting its empire in half at the Dardanelles by a seaborne assault, which would open up the Black Sea and relieve Russia. Churchill was soon converted and shelved his adventure around Borkum. As a seaborne operation it held out great possibilities of glory for the First Lord of the Admiralty. Fisher was much less enthusiastic, feeling that it would draw vital resources away from the North Sea, where he believed the significant naval clash must take place. Another naval loss—the battleship *Formidable*—had just occurred; torpedoed by the U24 in bright moonlight and stormy seas off Start Point in Devon, she sank with the loss of Captain Loxley and over 500 men. Bizarrely, one of the bodies washed ashore, Able Seaman John Cowan, laid out with others in the cellar of the 'Pilot Boat' pub in Lyme Regis, suddenly revived when the landlord's dog 'Lassie' licked and snuggled against him, providing a heart-warming story for the newspapers. Lloyd George also saw the Dardanelles plan as a chance for his own Adriatic adventure of 'knocking the props away' to be implemented. But he was distrustful of Churchill:

> Mr Churchill urged with all the inexorable force and pertinacity, together with the mastery of detail which he always commands when he is really interested in a subject, the merits of the Dardanelles scheme.

Lloyd George was attracted by Churchill's energy and restless enthusiasm; he admired his intellect but distrusted his judgement and was seriously irritated by his endless perorations in Cabinet, which wasted a lot of time and prevented other people getting a word in. 'If it wasn't for Winston's affectionate quality and good temper I sometimes think I can hardly do with him!' he told Margot Asquith, the Prime Minister's wife, who responded, 'Like all really self-centred people he ends by boring people. He's, as you say, such a child!' At this time Fisher was feeding letters revealing the tensions at the Admiralty around Churchill always wanting to do something 'big and striking'. Lloyd George finally showed his annoyance with Churchill when the latter interrupted him as he outlined his King's Pledge idea for limiting alcohol consumption, which was causing lost manufacturing production time. Churchill, who had no intention of giving up alcohol, objected, 'I don't see ...' but Lloyd George testily cut him short. 'You will see when you realise that conversation is not a monologue!' Later on that evening he apologised, but Churchill sat through the rest of the meeting red faced and in high dudgeon. He depended on the older man for support and the Cabinet status that support implied.

Fisher remained moodily silent during the Dardanelles discussions, but Kitchener came around when he heard that Churchill was prepared to go ahead with a purely naval expedition, at least to begin with. This meant that he could avoid parting with any precious troops for at least three months. Other ministers then followed Kitchener's lead. Clearly, some alternative strategy was required and Kitchener had opted for the one that seemed least likely to cause him much bother. When Fisher suddenly jumped up and made for the door, Kitchener followed him and after a whispered discussion by a window, persuaded the reluctant admiral back to the Council table.

Now into his sixties, Kitchener was beginning to look elderly. He lived in Carlton Gardens, with his military secretary and former ADC, the dapper Fitzgerald, promoted to colonel. Churchill had had rows with the War Office over the development of armoured cars and the prototype tank, and Lloyd George had clashed with Kitchener on a number of occasions, particularly about Welsh soldiers being banned from speaking Welsh, lack of nonconformist padres in the Army, and Kitchener's refusal to form a Welsh Division—all of which he backed down over when tackled by the fiery little attorney. He even appointed Lloyd George's nominee, Col. Owen Thomas, as general commanding the North Wales Brigade. 'Would you like to be a general?' the Field Marshal asked a startled Thomas when they met. 'Of course he would!' snapped Lloyd George. 'Well, I'll promote you to Brigadier General,' said Kitchener, reaching for his pen.

He was less accommodating with John Redmond, the nationalist leader, over the Irish Division being recruited among nationalists who were told that this was the best way to ensure a future for Home Rule after the war. Although Ulster volunteers and loyalists recruited in the north were allowed to have the red hand of Ulster as their flag and crest, nationalists were denied the harp as their emblem, although Kitchener as a concession suggested a shamrock shoulder flash. He was also prejudiced against the quarter-of-a-million-strong Territorial battalions raised before the war as a result of Haldane's reforms at the War Office, believing them to be ill-disciplined and improperly trained. He equated them with the civilian levies he had seen perform so badly in the Franco-Prussian war of his youth. These men went on to prove that they were just as good as his own Kitchener Volunteer battalions, and Territorial soldiers served in all theatres of the war with distinction.

Kitchener's style of improvisation, and trying to do everything himself, was wearing him down inexorably with the colossal volume of work. Articulate men like Lloyd George just could not understand him:

> I saw Lord Kitchener only on very rare occasions. At that date the War Lords were very exclusive and kept very much to themselves. They were both very busy [...] There was an impression that the military authorities thought it better we should not be told too much.

Indeed, in private Kitchener had said so. 'Everything revealed about war strategy in Cabinet is repeated by Ministers to their wives,' he said, but in Asquith's case it was 'revealed to other people's wives'. During this titanic conflict the Prime Minister was conducting a passionate and prolific correspondence with Venetia Stanley, a young woman his daughter Violet's age. He also had a reputation for fondling ladies hands at dinners and concerts after imbibing freely and placing them where they should not go. Even Churchill, no teetotaller, remarked to Clemmie: 'I like the old buffer, but it is a scandal.' Asquith on his part both liked and defended Churchill and Kitchener.

Kitchener was proud of his volunteers—a much higher calibre of men than normal army recruits. They were better educated, better fed, fitter, came from all walks of life, and were keen to learn. 'They became soldiers in spirit overnight,' recalled an officer who helped train them. However, the Field Marshal was having difficulty reconciling himself to the long casualty lists arriving from the Front. 'This isn't war!' he would exclaim, and inveigh against commanders squandering men's lives in futile attacks on heavy German defences. 'I will not have soldiers murdered!' he cried.

Early in 1915, the first Kitchener Volunteers marched to the great southern army base at Aldershot Camp to complete their training. One of them, George Coppard, recalled that Kitchener was to inspect them as they marched past in full kit:

> We were ordered to make a model salute and get the colour of Kitchener's eyes. On the command 'Eyes right!' I swung my head smartly and stared searchingly into the grey eyes. I was disappointed for they were so heavily hooded. In his greatcoat Kitchener looked very big, but so baggy and grey—nothing like the dark handsome posters of him which were displayed all over the country [...] We represented some of the earliest members of Kitchener's New Army of 70 divisions.

Lloyd George, who had likened Kitchener to a great revolving lighthouse that flashed light deep into the surrounding gloom then relapsed into complete darkness, described one such occasion in January 1915:

> At a meeting of the War Council Lord Kitchener had one more of those flashes which

now and again cast their rays deep into the gloom of the stormy problems which were raging around us. He said that he was impressed by the advantages which Germany derived from her central position. This enabled the enemy to co-ordinate their efforts. The Allies on the other hand were all acting independently. In his opinion there should be some central authority where all the Allies were represented and full information was available. Attacks should be arranged to take place simultaneously [...] I was entirely in favour of Lord Kitchener's suggestion, and I said that I was going to Paris shortly to meet the finance minister of the Allies.

This was an idea that at the time fell on stony ground, as Joffre did not wish to weaken his control of the battlefront, but it was one that Lloyd George remembered and resurrected at a later date when its originator was dead. The conceptual credit he later claimed entirely himself.

Early one January morning, as light began to grow over the chill North Sea, Churchill, Fisher and Admiral Wilson were all in the Admiralty War Room expecting a momentous engagement near the Dogger Bank. The German High Seas Fleet were known through decoded transcripts to be attempting another raid on the British coast. Royal Navy ships had been stealthily instructed to intercept the raiders. Churchill recalled:

There can be few purely mental experiences more charged with cold excitement than to follow, almost from minute to minute, the phases of a great naval action from the silent rooms of the Admiralty.

British battleships gathered near the Dogger Bank. Soon battlecruisers of Admiral Hipper's squadron were sighted and a stern chase saw Admiral David Beatty's ships open fire on the fleeing Germans at long range. One, the *Blücher*, lagged behind and was hit multiple times. Unfortunately, Beatty's ship the *Lion* was also disabled by fire from the two nearest German ships. Falling out of the chase, she sent signals that were misinterpreted by the pursuing ships, which left the fleeing enemy, among which was a badly damaged *Seydlitz*, Hipper's flagship, in order to concentrate fire on the doomed *Blücher*.

All this was relayed in snatches to the War Room. Churchill wrote:

Out on the blue water in the fighting ships amid the stunning detonations of the cannonade, fractions of the event unfold themselves to the corporeal eye. There is the sense of action at its highest; there is the wrath of battle; there is the intense self effacing, physical or mental toil. But in Whitehall only the clock ticks, and quiet men enter with quick steps laying slips of pencilled paper before other men equally silent, who draw lines and scribble calculations, and point with the finger or make brief subdued comments.

Scores of ships on both sides, including numerous destroyers and light cruisers, had been engaged in the chase, alert for mines and submarine hazards. *Lion*'s long-range shot had wrecked the stern and two rear gun turrets of the *Seydlitz* and had started a fire that burned down the hoist to the ammunition handling room and could have ignited the magazine had the officer not quickly flooded it. Unlike the British, the Germans learned a lesson from this. Fire screens and safety doors between the ammunition supply and the fighting turrets were often left open to aid the fast firing of guns. The British were to pay a heavy price at Jutland for the open train from the turret to the magazine. They also failed to learn from the deficiencies in their signalling system, still carried out using flag hoists and searchlight semaphore. Overestimates of the destruction wrought by their heavy armour-piercing shells were also made. The explosive nosecone in these often failed to penetrate the thick Krupp armour plate. A survivor from the *Blücher* reported the effects of the British shells exploding in the hold. 'Men were picked up by the terrific air pressure and tossed to a horrible death among the machinery.' Only six British heavy shells landed on the German battlecruisers, excluding the wretched *Blücher*, which was pounded until it sank. Over thirty German heavy shells hit the British ships, leading admirals to suspect that German gunnery was superior.

As the British circled, the *Blücher* turned turtle and hundreds of sailors swarmed over the handrails onto the whale-like hull, falling and jumping into the icy waters rising towards them. Of 1,200 crew, just 250 were plucked from the waves, the rescue operations hampered by the arrival of a German seaplane and a Zeppelin that started to shower bombs onto the stationary ships trying to take on board survivors.

Churchill drew a favourable comparison between Beatty's handling of the dramatic action and the performance of the generals on land:

> The Admiral actually leads the fleet in person and is probably under as severe fire and in as great danger as any man in it; a General [...] remains in his headquarters in complete tranquillity, ten, fifteen, or even twenty miles away. The phases of a naval action succeed one another at intervals of two or three minutes; whereas in modern battles two or three hours, or even days, elapse before fresh decisions are required from an Army Commander. [...] The Admiral's orders uttered from minute to minute are recorded for ever in the log book of every vessel engaged.

He observed that an army chief had a hundred ways of explaining a defeat on land and obscuring the consequences of his mistakes—such as continuing the attack the next day from a different direction. 'But on the sea no chance returns. The enemy disappears and the battle is over.' Despite this, some of the lessons that should have been learned from the successful tactical victory of Dogger Bank were not translated into success at the far greater naval battle yet to come. And Churchill's latter criticism of generals was by no means apparent in his relations with Sir John French, still commander of the BEF, who was very happy to share the hospitality of his 'tranquil' chateau at St Omer whenever Churchill visited.

Kitchener had been coming in for increasing criticism over the shortage of shells. Repeated requests for much more ammunition had been pouring into the War Office since September 1914 from the hard-pressed BEF. 'In view of the large expenditure of howitzer ammunition now taking place and to be expected, this is a serious matter. No effort should be spared to send out further supplies at once,' wired Sir John French. Later in the month, field gun ammunition was also very low. 'We have less than seven rounds per gun per day. This is far too small an amount.'

Meanwhile, the Germans were bombarding with giant high-explosive shells fired from much larger guns, in apparently limitless supply, nicknamed by the troops 'coalboxes'. Sir John received only prevaricating replies from the War Office and Board of Ordnance, which so far had been unable to find sufficient manufacturers to meet even the inadequate supplies they planned to provide. He reiterated, 'It is on the supply of ammunition for artillery that the future operations of the British Army will depend.' Lloyd George claimed in his memoirs that the Cabinet knew nothing of these urgent requests from their commander-in-chief at the time. Kitchener kept all War Office operations shrouded in secrecy, giving away little at Cabinet briefings.

Lloyd George started pushing for a Munitions Committee to put a rocket under the War Office. Kitchener, bogged down in a whole multitude of tasks, saw this as another burden that could only hinder. He had just announced that of 481,000 high-explosive shells ordered for the first quarter of 1915, only 52,000 would be delivered on time. He also rounded on Lloyd George for revealing to the new Munitions Committee the number of men sent to France that month. Lloyd George in turn said it was essential to know, so that sufficient guns and ammunition could be sent out. Days later he persuaded Kitchener to announce in Parliament how many men had been sent as reinforcements in order to appease Opposition demands for action on recruiting and ammunition! Despite the appointment of businessmen to assist him, Kitchener was floundering in the morass of armaments production. He confessed to a friend, 'The people here do not understand me, and I do not understand them.' Kitchener and King George V had accepted Lloyd George's pledge to abstain from alcohol for the duration of the war, and the result was that Kitchener began to put on weight, as it was observed that he ate more, instead of drinking his usual moderate amounts of wine or brandy. Neither Churchill nor Lloyd George bothered to observe the pledge.

As the new reinforcements started to feed into the Western Front, the British line was extended into France. By March, Sir John French was ready to launch a major offensive at Neuve Chapelle, which he expected to be a decisive battle. About 40,000 Allied troops, including Indian and British divisions, were launched against the German defences and thanks to excellent aerial photography beforehand and air superiority over the battlefield, they began to break through. The Indian divisions did well, capturing the objective of Aubers, despite inadequate artillery support that saw 1,000 of them shot down before they reached the trenches. Rifleman Gabbar Singh Negi of the 39th Garhwal Rifles led a bomb and bayonet party down the main German trench and went around each traverse first, clearing it of enemy before finally being killed. He was awarded the VC. But despite the advance, which ironed out a bulge in the Allied line, only a mile or two of ground was captured at a cost of about 11,000 casualties on both sides. Lloyd George described Kitchener striding into Cabinet:

> As soon as he sat down he exclaimed in husky tones—'Oh it is terrible, terrible!' We inquired if the casualties were very heavy. 'I'm not thinking of the casualties just now,' he said, 'but all the shells that were wasted!'

A later German counter-attack was aided by their use of poison gas. Heavier than air clouds of yellow-green chlorine drifted towards the Allied line, filling shell holes, then trenches and dugouts. Parts of the Indian divisions were first to be affected, and soldiers leaping from cover to escape the gas were mown down by concentrated machine-gun and rifle fire.

It was a new and terrible weapon, developed by fine scientific minds for the sole purpose of brutal extermination—the Germans codenamed it de-infestation. Soldiers and civilians in the path of the cloud found moist tissue such as the eyes, mouth and lungs were quickly racked with excruciating pain, as the chemical formed acid on contact which began to burn their flesh. Soldiers choked on searing fluid in their lungs, and corpses quickly turned black, spreading terror. Men were stricken with blindness, and even those led to the rear who survived the initial attack could die of cancer later because of permanent tissue damage. The only defence to begin with was to urinate into a rag and tie it over the mouth and nose to partially neutralise the effect on the lungs, but it was difficult to fight so encumbered, and massive reinforcements were rushed up to fill the gaps. The Germans were slow to follow up the attacks, because they were unsure how effective their rudimentary gas masks would be at protecting the wearer.

Sir John French was calling for more shells. In an interview given to a war correspondent and published in *The Times* in late March he blamed the failure of the attack at Neuve Chapelle on insufficient ammunition for the artillery—yet in the first thirty minutes of the bombardment more shells had been expended than in the entire course of the Boer War. At the 2nd Battle of Ypres soon afterwards, the Germans used gas on a wider scale. Up to 70,000 British and French casualties, mainly from gas attack, outnumbered the German casualties by two to one. Most victims died within ten minutes, unable to breathe. It was not until later in the year that effective gas masks were issued to Allied troops, Kitchener taking personal interest in their development. Meanwhile, the brave new soldiers from the Dominion of Canada, fit young men raised on a healthy lifestyle, tied urine-soaked handkerchiefs over their faces and counter-attacked across no man's land, suffering appalling casualties. Dominion troops were quickly found to be among the best that Britain had at its disposal and were used repeatedly in assaults where other soldiers got bogged down, but the battles were to drag on inconclusively until 100,000 men had been sacrificed by mid-June.

Kitchener was still struggling with both the new Munitions Committee and the political attacks on himself and the Master-General of Ordnance, Von Donop, a slow and meticulous man who was unsuited to the task he now faced in producing enough shells, and was also dissipating energy over the wrangles surrounding the Dardanelles expedition. After the initial naval bombardments of the Turkish forts on the straits in February had gone well, the task force had encountered sudden insurmountable difficulties. Admiral Carden fell ill, several battleships hit mines, blew up and sank, submarines were lost, and a spy was captured by the Turks with valuable information on Allied plans. Lloyd George, in reluctantly agreeing to the plan, had commented that he hoped '… the Army will not be expected to pull the Navy's chestnuts out of the fire!' But that is exactly what happened.

A German commander-in-chief, Liman Von Sanders, was co-ordinating the Turkish defences with the help of German staff officers. Kitchener only reluctantly agreed to send the regular 29th Division to form part of a landing force, including fresh Australian and New Zealand ANZAC troops waiting in Egypt, plus the Royal Naval Division and a French division. Gen. Sir Ian Hamilton, a Boer War colleague, was to be in command. He described the scene as he entered Kitchener's office:

> I bade him good morning and walked up to his desk, where he went on writing like a graven image. After a moment he looked up and said in a matter of fact tone, 'We are sending a military force to support the fleet now at the Dardanelles and you are to have command.' At that moment K wished me to bow, leave the room and make a start as I did some thirteen years ago.

But Hamilton stayed and politely asked Kitchener as to his precise instructions and how these were to be carried out. 'He gave me curt answers at first, but he slowly broadened out, until no one could get a word in edgeways.' The landings were to be on the Gallipoli peninsula, a name that would become infamous in military history.

Lloyd George had remained sceptical over the chances of success. 'Winston has acted too impetuously regarding the Dardanelles. Things out there are not going well … He is an able fellow but very dangerous. He will not look at arguments on the other side.' The landings began in April, but were carried out so slowly that the Turks were able to reinforce the heights commanding the beaches. General Stopford, in charge at Suvla Bay, did not even leave his ship. When asked how it was proceeding he replied, 'They are ashore!'

Bad news from Gallipoli coincided with the defeat of Russian allies on the Eastern Front. In the West, attacks on Aubers Ridge by the BEF had expended massive amounts of shells, and a storm broke over Kitchener's head, fuelled by officers sent from the Front by General French and an article in *The Times* by Colonel Repington stating. 'The attacks were well planned and valiantly conducted. The infantry did splendidly ... but the want of an unlimited supply of high explosive was a fatal bar to our success.' Lord Northcliffe, the owner of *The Times*, in a scathing editorial demanded to know why the BEF was so badly supplied in comparison to the French Army. His other paper, the populist *Daily Mail*, was more forthright in its headline 'THE SHELLS SCANDAL and LORD KITCHENER'S TRAGIC BLUNDER'. They even suggested the unthinkable—that Kitchener should go!

The British public have a mind of their own, however. Shocked by the presumption of these papers against their hero, they rallied to his defence. Copies of both newspapers were publicly burned on the floor of the Stock Exchange, and a placard placed outside the offices of the *Daily Mail* stated 'The Allies of the Hun', as circulation plummeted. The King announced that Kitchener was to be made a Knight of the Garter, and privately urged Asquith to make him Supreme Commander of all British forces. However, Asquith was in no position to comply. Admiral Fisher had taken an opportunity to compound the government's difficulties by choosing to resign, and this time meaning it.

Churchill had initially thought that he could smooth the old admiral's ruffled feathers, but he received a final note from his erstwhile colleague, who now claimed to have opposed the Dardanelles operation all along, 'Please do not wish to see me. There is nothing I could say. I am determined not to.' Even Asquith's emollient soothing could not change the old man's almost hysterical distaste for Churchill, who had set about forming a new Board of Admiralty with Sir Arthur Wilson as First Sea Lord in Fisher's place. But when Churchill went to see Asquith in his Thames-side house at Sutton Courtenay he was curtly told, 'No this won't do! I have decided to form a new Ministry.' Violet Asquith, returning from a boating trip on the river, recalled seeing 'Winston standing at the bottom of the lawn on the river's brink looking like Napoleon at St Helena ... He was very low ... Poor Clemmie [also present] was certainly a good deal upset.'

A rash of shocks followed for Churchill. Lloyd George told him blandly, 'But my dear Churchill, you know I have said that the Dardanelles campaign was a great mistake, and that someone else should be put in your place!' Asquith made it clear that he could not stay at the Admiralty, and Churchill was asked if 'a command in France' would be acceptable. Several MPs wrote to the Prime Minister to express the opinion that Churchill was a menace in any government office and should go, and his former Conservative colleagues, as well as prominent Liberal ones, did not want him in any national coalition. Lloyd George claimed to have tried to get him the Viceroyship of India or the Colonial Office in the new administration, but privately Lloyd George told his mistress Frances Stevenson:

> When the war came, he saw in it the chance of glory for himself and has entered on a risky campaign without caring a straw for the misery and hardship it would bring to thousands, in the hope that he would prove to be the outstanding man in this war.

At the last minute it seemed as if the German High Seas Fleet might be coming out, but after a day and a night of intense interest and voluminous signalled instructions on deployments it all fizzled out and Churchill's glory days at the Admiralty were over—torpedoed by an ageing hulk! His judgement in men was always hit and miss. He was far too influenced by whether he warmed to a person, whether or not they excited him; in fact, whether they were rather like himself.

Asquith formed a National Coalition on 25 May, with the Conservative leader Bonar Law as Colonial Secretary and Arthur Balfour as First Lord of the Admiralty. Kitchener, of course, remained as Secretary for War. Lloyd George agreed to head up a new Ministry of Munitions, while Churchill got the Chancellorship of the Duchy of Lancaster, the lowest-ranking position in the Cabinet. He told Lord Riddell, proprietor of the *News of the World* (once a well-read newspaper), 'I am finished in respect of all I care for—the waging of war, the defeat of the Germans.'

He was bitter about what he saw as his friend Lloyd George's treachery:

> Lloyd George is responsible for the coalition government [...] Notwithstanding how I stood by him in Marconi days, he did nothing to help me [...] He acted just as if they were killing a rat [and] never hesitates to sacrifice a friend if he stands in the way of his game.

Churchill remained disgruntled and rebuffed Lloyd George's friendly overtures when they met in Cabinet. For some time he could not bring himself to speak directly to his former ally, but made his comments via others who happened to be present. He stated in a letter at this time, 'Between me and Lloyd George tout est fini' (all is finished). Fisher he simply called 'a treacherous devil'. Yet, some months later, he would strain credulity by advocating the old seadog's reinstatement at the Admiralty!

At first, Churchill was included with most of his old colleagues in the newly reconstituted Dardanelles Committee, the new name for the War Council, and continued to advocate reinforcing the Balkans. However, Lloyd George was more interested in a redirected thrust via Salonika, Churchill commenting to a new Conservative colleague, 'You see how much this man dominates the Cabinet!' But soon he was converted to play a part with Curzon, the former Viceroy, and Lloyd George in advocating conscription. Anathema to many Liberals as an invasion of individual liberty of conscience, the conscription issue became tied to a furtive movement to get rid of Kitchener from the War Office and replace him with Lloyd George, who had already taken on many of his responsibilities via the Ministry of Munitions. Churchill wrote of Lloyd George, 'He has the war-making quality. I do not intend to allow any personal feelings from preventing me working with him. But distrust based on experience is a terrible barrier.'

About this time Churchill also discovered a lifetime therapy in the practice of landscape painting. He stumbled on his sister-in-law Lady 'Goonie' Churchill

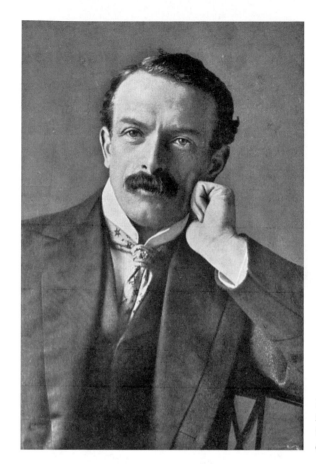

1 The Welsh Wizard in reflective pose. Lloyd George could charm and enchant his audience.

2 'Highgate', Llanystumdwy, and the attached cobbler's shop in the foreground where Lloyd George grew up.

3 Beloved Uncle Lloyd and his favourite nephew. Richard Lloyd heaped praise and encouragement on David.

4 The cottage-bred Prime Minister, with Lord Milner and Philip Kerr, walking the back roads of Llanystumdwy.

5 Happy family—Margaret and David with their youngest daughter Megan and eldest Mair, who was soon to die tragically young.

6 Roughneck republicans? Three sitting Welsh MPs and a Welsh clergyman planning independence.

7 A rare photo of Kitchener's mother, brother and sister with Kitchener as a baby.

8 A young Royal Engineer lieutenant who nearly lost his commission.

9 Palestine survey in 1875. Lt Kitchener is sprawled to the right of the tent, head on hand.

10 In a studio pose—Winston's beloved mother, Lady Randolph Churchill.

11 Radical dandy Lord Randolph Churchill could not be a duke so became a demagogue.

12 Winston in his tight
cavalry breeches and 4th
Hussars dress uniform,
1895.

13 Young Winston on
a favourite pony at
Bangalore, 1896.

14 Kitchener directing
Egyptian officers on
campaign.

15 Churchill as a young war
correspondent and officer
in the South African Light
Horse.

16 The folly of war. Churchill among prisoners at Pretoria (on right).

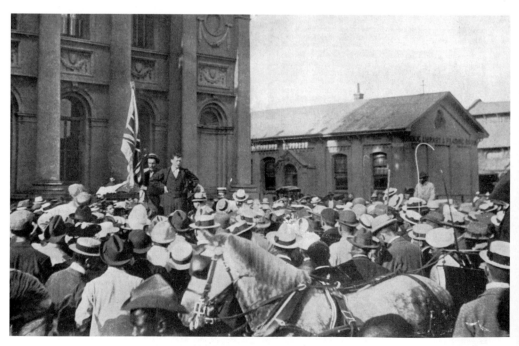

17 Churchill gives a speech on the steps of the town hall at Durban after his daring escape, 1899.

18 Officers watching the progress of the battle of Colenso from General Redvers Buller's headquarters on Naval Gun Hill, Second Boer War.

19 Mr Winston Churchill, the honourable member for Oldham, 1900.

20 Kitchener, despite the ferocity of his military methods, had always been willing to talk peace. Here he is seated at a peace conference at Vereeniging, south of Johannesburg, on 15 April 1902.

21 Kitchener's favourite ADC, Frank Maxwell, the son he never had.

22 Mentor and collaborator—a classic portrait of their relationship. Lloyd George strides confidently forward, while a deferential Churchill follows in his wake.

23 Warlord of all he surveys—Kaiser Wilhelm, wearing his imperial helmet, directs German Army manoeuvres watched by an eager Churchill in his Hussar uniform, 1908.

24 Liberal grandees Sir Edward Grey, Churchill and Lord Crewe flanked by police officers.

25 Lord Kitchener, now committed to his enormous task of raising the armies, with Sir Edward Grey in Paris.

26 Good-natured euphoria reigned in the queues outside recruiting stations set up throughout Britain.

27 Sir John French with a French general in Paris. Sir John became increasingly uneasy about conforming to the movements of the French Army.

28 Churchill haranguing a crowd on the war effort, accompanied by Clemmie in an impressive hat.

29 Lieutenant General Sir William Birdwood accompanying Field Marshal Lord Kitchener on a visit to Anzac, Gallipoli in November 1915. It was after this visit that Kitchener recommended the total evacuation of Gallipoli by British forces.

*Above:* 30 As the *Blücher* turns turtle, hundreds of sailors swarm over the hull. Her guns point to the sky before the final plunge into the icy depths.

*Right:* 31 Sir Douglas Haig and Marshal Joffre doing their best to convince Lloyd George during his visit to the battlefront during the Somme offensive, 1916.

*Above left:* 32 Aged just nineteen, Allan Cliffe joined the Army as a Kitchener Volunteer in his hometown of Huddersfield, Yorkshire.

*Above right:* 33 Lloyd George visited Asquith at his home with plans for a newly constituted war committee.

34 Churchill's resilient spirit helped sustain Lloyd George in his darkest hours.

35 Lloyd George meeting the soldiers. The quality of British troops was beginning to deteriorate thanks to reckless offensives.

*Above left:* 36 The Tiger and the Wizard—Clemenceau and Lloyd George.

*Above right:* 37 Lloyd George's chosen man—Marshal Foch, Supreme Commander of Allied Forces.

*Above:* 38 Chief of the General Staff Paul von Hindenburg, Kaiser Wilhelm II and General Erich Friedrich Wilhelm Ludendorff study maps of the front, November 1917.

*Left:* 39 Field Marshal Sir Henry Hughes Wilson was one of the most senior British Army staff officers of the First World War. He and General Ludendorff were opposing war planners.

*Below:* 40 Marshal Foch, Lloyd George and French Premier Briand, after the conclusion of hostilities.

painting in the garden of Hoe Farm in Surrey, the Churchill country hideaway of the time, out of reach of Zeppelin-infested London. She encouraged him to have a go and, after trying watercolours, he soon gained a proficiency in oils and produced many colourful views of an impressionistic style. It was 'the only occupation which he ever pursued in total silence' and proved a solace for his loss of a demanding Cabinet position.

The 50,000 casualties at the Battle of Loos without tangible result, and the increasing demand for troops in the Dardanelles, had created a manpower crisis. Kitchener was struggling with strategy on several fronts—in the West, on the Russian Front and in the Middle East. In August, it was decided to recall General Hamilton, who had been unsuccessful. Kitchener said to Asquith, 'I pace my room at night and rack my brain.' He liked Hamilton but could not afford to gamble more troops.

Meanwhile, Lloyd George was doing much to undermine Kitchener's authority. He had never liked or understood the taciturn soldier and suspected the efficiency of his methods. In one much quoted instance, he had sent a representative from the Ministry of Munitions, Eric Geddes, to ask how many machine guns would be required per battalion in nine months' time. 'Do you think that I am God Almighty, that I can tell you what will be wanted nine months ahead?' demanded Kitchener. 'No, sir,' said Geddes, 'and I do not think I am either, but we have to work it out between us and try to get it right!' Kitchener thought for a moment and then named a modest figure of a minimum of two and a maximum of four per battalion. He signed a chit, which Geddes showed to Lloyd George, who gaily multiplied the maximum to sixty-four. This quantity, however, was only ever obtained by the specialist Machine Gun Corps alone, by the end of the war, despite Lloyd George's boasting.

At a conference on munitions in France during September, Lloyd George conceived the need for a vastly increased heavy gun production schedule. The Army's representative, General Du Cane, backed him up, but Kitchener was furious. Accustomed all his life to frugality with materials of war, he decided he had to stop this prodigality in its tracks. In a letter from the War Office dated 1 October, he cancelled the order. He also circulated a memo to the Cabinet calling on them to judge between himself and Lloyd George. A committee was appointed to examine the matter, but it sat only once. 'I suppose that means the end of your programme,' J. T. Davies said to Lloyd George. 'No,' came the reply, 'it means the end of the committee.' The heavy gun programme was pushed through. 'Before I ceased to be Minister of Munitions, it turned out that even more guns were needed by our army than the large number which I had ordered,' wrote Lloyd George.

Asquith neutralised the situation somewhat by suggesting that Kitchener take a tour of the Gallipoli peninsula, and deal with the conscription issue by a system of attestation in which eligible men aged between 18 and 41 registered for service but were not called up unless needed. But this was simply cleverly disguising the inevitable. The Prime Minister himself took over at the War Office in Kitchener's absence, Lloyd George claiming to have a lump in his throat as Kitchener took his leave of the Cabinet. 'Not a word was spoken! He might have been going out to lunch.' More than one of his colleagues hoped that the old soldier might stop a bullet or hit a mine on his journey through the war zone, thus relieving them of a political impasse.

He disappointed them all by arriving safely in the Dardanelles, where he was greeted by his old ADC, now General Birdwood and commander of the ANZAC troops at Gallipoli. An unannounced tour in the front-line trenches brought spontaneous ovations of applause from the battle-hardened New Zealand and Australian soldiers, as Kitchener's unmistakable moustache and profile hove into view. Here was the great soldier come to view the conditions for himself and sharing the same dangers as themselves, yards from the enemy. He seemed at home with the Levantine sun glaring down on his sunburned features, as he eagerly viewed the Turkish positions by trench periscope and binoculars. 'I can't tell you how glad I am to have you with me again, Birdie, and to be away from all those bloody politicians,' he exclaimed. 'Thank God I came to see this for myself. I had no idea of the difficulties you were up against. I think you have all done wonders.' The soft underbelly, he now knew, was proving tough meat.

One who was unwilling to digest that fact found himself totally excluded from war decision-making. Asquith's next master stroke had been, like a headmaster separating troublesome pupils, to isolate Lloyd George as a potential threat by excluding Churchill from the new smaller War Committee just formed. As Asquith had probably foreseen, Churchill immediately offered to resign from the Cabinet:

> I could not accept a position of general responsibility for war policy without any effective share in its guidance and control [...] I therefore ask you to submit my resignation to the King. I am an officer and place myself unreservedly at the disposal of the military authorities.

So Churchill went to war, sharing the hardships and facing the dangers of the common run of men. Lloyd George wished him luck and betrayed a genuine sense of loss. He had been both his ally and the originator of snide Churchill-baiting comments, enjoyed by many who, like himself, resented the verbosity of their engaging but somewhat wearing and vainglorious colleague. Poking fun at and appreciating the value of a man's character are not inconsistent principles. Lloyd George was driving a full-out war effort at the Ministry of Munitions, stepping up output tremendously with the construction of government ordnance factories twelve miles long, complete with their own railway systems. But he had no intention of forgetting his colleague. Churchill would not rusticate in the trenches for long.

# 9

# Pillar of Sacrifice

Churchill was convinced that Kitchener's prevarication about sending out the 29th Division to Gallipoli had fatally delayed General Hamilton's attack until it was too late. He was equally convinced that he had been let down by the naval authorities who got cold feet about pressing the bombardment of Turkish forts in the narrows when they started to lose ships. 'I did not receive from the First Sea Lord either the clear guidance before the event, or the firm support after, which I was entitled to expect,' he had said of Fisher in his resignation speech to the House of Commons.

He found a sympathiser for his troubles in Sir John French, who sent a chauffeur-driven car to take him to GHQ at St Omer when he arrived in France. Sir John had grievances of his own against Kitchener and lent a ready ear to Churchill's brandy-fuelled complaints against the sphinx-like idol of the people. Sir John promised to get his important political friend and ally a brigade to command as soon as possible. In the meantime, he arranged for Churchill to be attached to the 2nd Battalion Grenadier Guards for familiarisation with trench warfare. After the first shock of wading through flooded trenches and making the acquaintance of the rats that lived alongside the men, he discovered that sixteen years of luxury since the South African War had 'in no way impaired the tone of my system'. His new colonel, George Jeffreys, was not thrilled to have him. 'I think you ought to know that we were not at all consulted in the matter of your coming to join us.' Soon Churchill was writing to Clemmie for a warm leather waistcoat and trench wading boots, a periscope (most important), and a sheepskin sleeping bag, shortly supplemented by demands for more alcohol and food.

He was impressed by the strict discipline of the Guards and their indifference to casualties. 'What has to be done is done and the losses accepted without fuss or comment.' They also became impressed by Churchill's seriousness, and ready endurance of danger or hardship. Jeffreys so far relented as to offer to make Churchill his second-in-command. By early December he had been told he was to command a brigade comprising four Lancashire battalions and asked Clemmie to order him a new brigadier-general's tunic. But when French broached the subject on a visit to London with the Prime Minister, a political storm threatened. French was on his way out. The truculent commander-in-chief having meddled with ministers over the shells crisis, Asquith had determined to replace him with Sir Douglas Haig. Asquith let slip a phrase that rankled with Churchill when he heard it. 'Perhaps you might give him a battalion?'

All Churchill's previous good humour—'I have found happiness and content such as I have not known for many months … they all say I look five years younger!'— soon evaporated. He brooded in his dugout. Who were they to dispose the fate of a brilliant man like him? The sour tone of his letters to Clemmie betrayed his overriding obsession. 'The hour of Asquith's punishment and K's exposure draws nearer. The wretched men have nearly wrecked our chances. It may fall to me to strike the blow. I shall do it without compunction.' But she wisely advocated caution, discretion and keeping his political options open. Clemmie remained on good terms with the Asquiths, visiting and acting as her husband's advocate in London among the chattering classes who wielded power in the background. Asquith's daughter Violet, now Mrs Bonham Carter, was still a firm Churchill admirer, but his wife Margot was more lukewarm. Clemmie seriously distrusted Lloyd George, 'fair of speech, shifty of eye, treacherous of heart …' as she described him, but Churchill was a believer in *realpolitik* and realised that the two mavericks needed one another. 'If I were killed Asquith would be sorry, but it would suit his political hand. Lloyd George would not be sorry, but it would not suit his political hand at all.' But for the moment, Churchill's political stock was very low indeed.

In December, Churchill said goodbye to Sir John French after a procession of generals had said their final farewells to the departing chief at GHQ. The previous day the two men had picnicked in a pretty Flanders cottage, and now the retiring field marshal spent his last quarter of an hour with the fallen minister. Churchill made a few tours of the French troops adjacent and was presented with a *poilu*'s blue steel helmet, which he wore as a distinctive piece of practical headgear 'to protect my valuable cranium'. However, it was the dark Glengarry cap of his new regiment that he wore as he arrived, mounted on a black charger, to take command as colonel of his new battalion, the 6th Royal Scots Fusiliers, accompanied by his second-in-command Archie Sinclair and two grooms with a pile of luggage, all equally well mounted on thoroughbred horses. After summoning the officers to lunch, during which he mainly scowled at them in silence, he made a short speech promising that 'those who support me I will look after. Those who go against me I will break.' He then paraded the men and attempted a drill, using archaic cavalry commands (although this was an infantry regiment).

The result was predictable, and so soon after the devastating losses of the battle of Loos. He wrote to Clemmie:

> This regiment is pathetic. The young officers are all small middle class Scotsmen, very brave and intelligent, but obviously quite new to soldiering. All the seniors and all the professionals have fallen [he might have added that tall men make better targets]. I believe I shall be a help to them.

And so it proved.

In the House of Commons, Lloyd George had chosen the end of the year to give his considered opinion of the 'muddled campaign of 1915':

> Too late in moving here, too late in arriving there, too late in coming to this decision, too late in starting enterprises, too late in preparing! In this war the footsteps of the allied forces have been dogged by the mocking spectre of 'too late' and unless we quicken our movements, damnation will fall on the sacred cause for which so much gallant blood has flowed ...

He was criticising the conduct of the war, and by implication the government of which he was a prominent member. In fact, he was feeling depressed and toying with the idea of resigning and forming an Opposition with Churchill and the Unionist politician Edward Carson, who had resigned earlier.

But Lloyd George was not merely a critic; he had been putting his creative and practical skills to good use at the Ministry of Munitions. He had championed the establishment of a machine-gun training centre and cleared the red tape that was preventing 10,000 men being put continuously under instruction in their devastating use. Lloyd George estimated that 'the most lethal weapon of the war' was equivalent, with its ten-man team, of at least the killing power of fifty riflemen. At the end of 1915, just over 6,000 machine guns had been manufactured; in the following year the output shot up to 33,500 and continued to double annually. He rushed through the approval and manufacture of the Stokes trench mortar, designed by Wilfred Stokes, an agricultural machinery manufacturer from East Anglia. It quickly fired bombs into enemy trenches simply by loading them into an upright steel tube, but the War Office had not approved the type of fuse on the propellant charge. The Army was clamouring for such a weapon, and it became a standard design around the world.

After Churchill's authorisation of an experimental tank, Lloyd George picked up the tab when he saw trials of a prototype machine and arranged for the Ministry of Munitions to begin manufacture. In February 1916, the first demonstration of the 'mother' tank took place at Hatfield Park. HMS *Centipede* (it had been developed by the Navy) crawled through thick entanglements and wallowed over deep mud, parapets and trenches. Kitchener, who was present, scoffed and said artillery would soon knock it out, but privately he told Gen. Sir William Robertson, his new Chief of the Imperial General Staff (CIGS), that it was far too valuable a weapon to have been shown openly to so many spectators, including garrulous politicians, and that its tactical surprise value might be lost through careless talk. He kept a keen eye on its development.

Filled shell production had tripled to 238,000 per week by January 1916 from the figure when Lloyd George took over at Munitions, that figure quadrupling by midsummer, and the amount of artillery of all types manufactured increased fivefold.

There were unsung heroes of the munitions industry, particularly the women who engaged in war work at the new filling factories that sprang up all over the country. Toxic jaundice could result from TNT poisoning, as the chemicals had to be poured in by hand, their bright yellow faces earning them the sobriquet of 'canaries' from their contemporaries. The danger of explosion was ever present, and the one at Hayes in Middlesex was heard by millions. Colonel Lee, a representative of Lloyd George, visited the scene where he met a white-faced, busy little woman about 5 feet tall who was in charge of the workers. 'Is this where the explosion took place?' he asked. As he entered he saw bloodstains on the floor and all the survivors carrying on at full speed. The forewoman had calmed her girls and headed them back to their dangerous task. 'When I think of those poor boys in France who are facing more dangers than we are here,' she said, 'I am not going to run away.' Defying death and mutilation, the women sang songs of their own composition to keep up their spirits, 'which had little perhaps of literary grace, but plenty of crude vigour and unfaltering courage' wrote Lloyd George.

On his return from the Dardanelles, Kitchener had tendered his resignation to Asquith, but it was not accepted. Asquith told him that they should stick together in the face of Cabinet criticism and soldier on, and a plan for evacuating the Gallipoli peninsula with minimum casualties was contrived. Secretly, Asquith hoped that his recent appointment of Sir William Robertson, a sound organiser of logistics, would circumvent Kitchener's authority and appease his most ardent critics in the government like Lloyd George, as well as those outside it. Robertson made sure he came to a firm agreement with Kitchener about their respective roles and drew up a memorandum which both men signed. Kitchener was reassured. 'I have utmost confidence in his loyal support on sometimes difficult occasions owing to political interference, and I am sure we will get on well together.' The new CIGS had come up the hard way, enlisting as a private trooper in 1877, and was an ally of the new commander-in-chief Douglas Haig. The two men knew and trusted one another, and believed in total commitment to the Western Front without distracting 'sideshows'.

Robertson's first act was to order the evacuation of Cape Helles, the last bastion of the Gallipoli peninsula held by British forces. The Turks were fooled by various means into thinking that the troops were still there until the last got off safely. 'It will be up to date and probably into all eternity as sordid and miserable a chapter of amateur enterprise as ever was written in our history,' wrote Lord Lovat of the Lovat Scouts, a famous reconnaissance unit. Despite this débâcle and lack of progress in France, Kitchener never lost the esteem of the British public. He was the supreme war leader and the symbol of the Empire's unity of purpose. He told Douglas Haig, 'Rightly or wrongly, probably wrongly, the people believe in me. It is not me the politicians are afraid of, but what the people would say to them if I were to go.'

Kitchener now spent more spare time at Broome Park, a country house in Kent he had bought for his retirement, where he enjoyed directing alterations and improvements and working in the gardens. The grounds were used as a recuperation camp for wounded soldiers, and he relaxed in their company, talking to them about their experiences. He had lost many of his old comrades, including his favourite former ADC Frank Maxwell, who had been killed leading an attack on German lines during the summer of 1915. The officer classes were sustaining very high casualties, and things would only get worse. Lady Desborough replied to Kitchener's anguished letter of regret over the death of both her officer sons:

> My dear Lord K, my dear friend. You were always so good to Julian and Billy. I seem often to see them walking on each side of you at Wrest when they were very young [...] I am writing to say that you must not grieve for us.

Along with Robertson and Haig, Kitchener soon found himself committed to a planned offensive in the area of the Somme on the Western Front, scheduled for early summer 1916. General Joffre was confident that with the thirty-eight divisions the British now had in line, plus nineteen expected by the summer, the Allies would have with the French and Belgian armies a numerical superiority over the Germans of 139 divisions to 117. Kitchener advised Haig to 'husband the strength' of the British Army, but he also enthusiastically ordered the construction of fifty tanks to assist the attack and supported the development along with the Navy of a large aircraft capable of carrying a 3-inch bore gun able to shoot down Zeppelins as well as carry a bomb load. The Germans pre-empted the Allied plan by attacking the French fortress of Verdun in February, seizing the initiative, always an advantage in war. It was not a vital position, but French pride would not allow its relinquishment and the battle drained French resources, spawned the slogan 'They shall not pass', and made the name of the defender, General Pétain. It ate up 315,000 French casualties, seriously affecting morale, and thus weakened the summer offensive, as the German High Command intended, but drained German resources too.

At the end of January 1916, Churchill led his rested and retrained battalion back into line at Ploegsteert, one of the less busy sectors, but lively enough. There was sporadic shelling, and he organised adventures into no man's land to test the enemy defences. As the whizz-bangs flew overhead, he enthused to a fellow officer, 'I do love war!' But blacker moments came when he heard of the successful trials of the caterpillar tank. He wrote to Clemmie:

> Are they not fools not to use my mind—or knaves to wait for its destruction by some flying splinter? I do not fear death or wounds and I like the daily life out here, but their impudence and complaisance make me quite spiteful at times.

For five weeks he endured the day-to-day life of the trenches until the call of parliamentary business drew him back on leave. He had meetings with Lloyd George, among others, on the need for an effective prosecution of the war and a regrouping of the talents either in Opposition or as an alternative government. Lloyd George told his brother:

> Winston wants to come back from the army. He is a brilliant but a most unreliable fellow [...] he wants to return from his dreary trenches. Sorry for him. A brilliant fellow without judgement which is adequate to his fiery impulse. His steering gear is too weak for his horsepower.

Churchill had much the worst of an exchange with Arthur Balfour, the new First Lord of the Admiralty, when, after a masterful summary of the military situation, Churchill astounded parliamentary colleagues by suggesting that Fisher be reinstated as First Sea Lord. Arrogantly, he left the chamber immediately after his speech and did not hear the reply by Admiral of the Fleet, Sir Hedworth Meux MP, who asked what the current First Sea Lord had done to merit summary replacement?

> In the first few months of the war whenever we had a success, or whenever the enemy had a slight failure, the whole of the Navy were pained by the vulgar boasting that went on [...] anyone in the Navy knows what an unlucky thing it is to boast. [...] we all wish the former First Lord a great deal of success in France, and we hope that he will stay there.

The next day Balfour piled on his own scorn. 'I cannot follow the workings of the Rt. Hon. Gentleman's mind. Was he advocating the very man who after five months refused to work with him, who the Rt. Hon. Gentleman said did not give him either the guidance or support to which he was entitled?' Churchill's attempt to explain did not help, and he returned to France seething with frustration. What he thought would be seen as a magnanimous conciliatory gesture to a talented ex-colleague, at last eager for employment again, was interpreted as the ravings of a mind unhinged by thwarted ambition. But whatever his state of mind, the men at the front liked him. His adjutant, A. D. Gibb said:

> He is a man who is apparently always to have enemies. He made none in his regiment, but left behind him there men who will always be his loyal partisans and admirers, and who are proud of having served in the Great War under the leadership of one who is beyond question a great man.

Perhaps this opinion, born out of the mud and blood of the trenches where much that is insincere and insubstantial in human relations falls away, counted for something in Churchill's mind.

He did not know whether to resign his commission and return to Parliament, writing to various colleagues to seek their advice. Clemmie urged patience and added a plea of her own:

When next I see you I hope there will be a little time for us both alone. We are still young, but time flies, stealing love away and leaving only friendship which is very peaceful but not very stimulating or warming.

By late April there were hints that Churchill might get his much longed for brigade, but he had made up his mind to return. Kitchener warned him, however, that he could leave the Army, but he must not change his mind again and could never return. In early May his regiment was amalgamated and a senior colonel replaced him as CO. He gave his officers a memorable farewell luncheon in Armentières and, leaving his front-line military career behind, returned to London and destiny.

At the end of May and on the first day of June 1916 was fought the battle for which all Britain and the world had been waiting since the beginning of the war. England's Glory, the Royal Navy, finally had the chance to confront and annihilate the German High Seas Fleet. Superior in their numbers of ships and range of guns, if Britain's Grand Fleet could get to grips with the enemy the result seemed certain. The Admiralty had picked up vastly increased radio traffic, which told them that the German fleet was putting to sea. The German plan was to lure a small portion of the British fleet to destruction by superior numbers after sending fast cruisers to either bombard the English coast or interfere with shipping. A battlecruiser squadron might be destroyed and the odds evened between the relative size of the two main fleets before an all-out fleet action.

Sir John Jellicoe, the Admiral in charge of the Grand Fleet anchored at Scapa Flow in the Orkneys, was well aware of this. 'He is the only man on either side who can lose the war in one day,' said Churchill. German submarines had been sent ahead to be ready for the approach of British ships, but they were outguessed by the experienced British naval tacticians, who ordered the 2nd and 5th Battlecruiser Squadrons out of their Scottish bases earlier than the Germans had expected, and the Grand Fleet had already upped anchor and was heading out of Scapa Flow before the German fleet was at sea.

Admiral Beatty's light cruisers were soon in action with Hipper's battlecruisers off the coast of Jutland. A confused fight ensued in which again, as at Dogger Bank, Beatty's radio masts aboard his flagship *Lion* were soon shot away and he was reduced to signalling by flag hoist and lamps, which were difficult to read in the smoke of battle. As soon as he sighted the approach of the German main fleet he turned to the north and ran directly towards Jellicoe and the Grand Fleet, who were steaming towards the gunfire. Before they came in sight, Beatty edged to the east, drawing the Germans into a disadvantageous position to return fire against the approaching Grand Fleet. Steaming line abreast, row after row of gigantic steel gun platforms pouring smoke from their funnels as they ploughed at high speed through the increasing haze, the fleet had now to deploy in a sweeping arc to encompass the retreating battle squadrons and enfold the enemy in a deadly embrace of fire.

The German commander, Admiral Reinhard Scheer, wrote:

It was now obvious that we were confronted by a large portion of the enemy fleet. The entire arc stretching from north to east was a sea of fire. The flash from the muzzles of guns was seen distinctly through the mist and smoke on the horizon, although the ships themselves were not distinguishable.

A deadly dance followed, with the German fleet attempting to elude their massed foe—151 British ships to a mere ninety-nine German vessels. Throughout the night the manoeuvres continued until the Germans were able to punch through the light cruiser screen to the north of the Grand Fleet standing between them and home. Ship after ship was damaged and sunk, but it was becoming apparent that German armour was stronger than the British counterpart, and that German shells were more effective. By dawn, British ships looked on seas cleared of the enemy, but 6,000 seamen and 112,000 tons of shipping had been lost, while the German losses were roughly half that. The Grand Fleet, however, was still dominant. One month after Jutland, its numbers were replenished by new ships and men.

Beatty's comment that 'there is something wrong with our ships and something wrong with our system' was echoed by a naval inquiry, which made changes in signalling, fleet standing orders to allow more initiative to captains, gunnery targeting and in particular ammunition handling practices—which had led to catastrophic explosions after hits ignited the supply chain, blowing up the magazine and sinking five major warships. Jutland was neither a defeat nor a victory for either side, but it convinced German admirals that wearing down the Royal Navy by attrition in fleet actions was not an option, and the British that they had to change operational procedures and improve armaments.

Days later a further battlecruiser, HMS *Hampshire*, damaged at Jutland, was sunk by a mine released by a U-boat off the Orkneys. It rated as one of the biggest disasters of the war, not only for the loss of the ship and crew but because of the famous soldier who had taken passage on her *en route* for Russia only that morning.

Kitchener had been increasingly involved in controversy. Asquith had utilised him as a bomb shelter against politicians who wanted universal conscription, led by those like Lloyd George who believed in a knockout war to the finish. Kitchener had stuck by the idea of using only volunteers as long as he could, but the tide proved too strong to resist. In answer to his general critics he strode down to Parliament and at a public briefing open to all members he departed from his usual taciturnity to give a masterful presentation and appraisal of the war, its problems and how he had dealt with them. Wearing his blue Royal Engineers uniform, he drew applause by his performance and answered questions with assurance and geniality. The following day he lunched with the King, who was delighted at his success and wished him well on a secret mission.

Russia had been in trouble for some time, needing money, armaments and strategic assistance to maintain the Eastern Front. Kitchener was now to go, at the invitation of the Czar, on a top-level diplomatic mission to review the situation. Originally it had also been intended to send Lloyd George to discuss munitions, but he was now tied up with the problems following the Easter Rising in Dublin, following which fifteen Irish nationalists had been shot by a British firing squad, leading to widespread fury in Ireland. The frustrations of this task would further depress the fiery Welsh attorney.

On the other hand, Kitchener seemed light-hearted and 'as merry as a schoolboy' when packing for his Russian trip. Just a shadow of sadness passed his features briefly as he bade farewell from the railway carriage window. 'Look after things while I am away,' were his last words. Then he was off, heading north for Thurso, where the destroyer HMS *Oak* was waiting to carry him to Scapa Flow in the Orkneys. The corkscrewing motion of the small ship in a north-easterly gale lashing the Pentland Firth was an unpleasant experience for Kitchener and his staff. Not only was he an indifferent sailor at the best of times, but the compound fracture in his leg sustained when he fell from his horse in India troubled him in wet weather. With the aid of a stick he crossed the narrow, swaying gangway slung between the tiny *Oak* and Admiral Jellicoe's towering flagship *Iron Duke*, at anchor in Scapa Flow. Ships were still returning from the battle at Jutland, and all was activity as they were refuelled and damage was attended to. At lunch with Jellicoe, talk ranged over the inconclusive battle, and Kitchener pondered if it could be considered a British victory.

The Secretary for War was then transferred to HMS *Hampshire*, which set out with a destroyer escort of two ships, intended to ward off submarines. Unfortunately, the storm had swung to the north-west, and their route to the west of the Orkneys meant that the ships were encountering very heavy seas that drove them towards a jagged shore of towering black cliffs. Having fallen behind the more powerful *Hampshire*, the two destroyers were ordered back to base. Suddenly a terrific explosion rent the battlecruiser and all the lights went out. She had just struck a mine laid by a lone U-boat days before, and was now rapidly settling by the bows and heeling over to starboard. Kitchener was escorted to the bridge, appearing calm and unruffled to eyewitnesses. He stood on the storm-lashed quarterdeck in his khaki tunic, giving instructions to his military staff. Captain Savill called for him to enter a lifeboat, but no one saw him do so. In the event, it made no difference, as only three cork rafts got away from the ship and few survived the rigorous crossing to the rocky shore. The *Hampshire* sank within fifteen minutes, taking all the lifeboats with her. Most of the officers and men who had come unscathed through Jutland, where they had sunk a cruiser and two submarines, perished with the ship alongside the icon of the British Empire. For Field Marshal the Earl Kitchener of Khartoum, Secretary of State for War, who had spent his life in sunburnt lands, died in just the sort of cold wet weather conditions he passionately loathed.

Balfour, First Lord of the Admiralty, had asked Churchill to help him draft a more reassuring bulletin following his disastrous decision to tell the bald truth about British losses in the Battle of Jutland that had resulted in a burst of public and media hysteria. Churchill was using his journalistic talents to seriously fudge the issue when it was knocked off the front pages by the announcement of the loss of the *Hampshire* and the death of Kitchener. Coming out of the blue, it was a politician's godsend. 'The old man couldn't have chosen a better moment to go,' declared C. P. Scott, editor of *The Manchester Guardian*, and Churchill, sitting in the Athenaeum Club with General Hamilton bemoaning their misfortunes at Gallipoli, on hearing the news shouted in the street below, agreed that Kitchener had died 'at the right time in his life'. Not to be outdone in memorable statements, Lloyd George dramatically declared that his Cabinet colleagues 'had Kitchener's blood on their hands', although not particularly singling himself out for blame. He wrote:

> On the 6th day of June 1916, I walked across from the Ministry of Munitions to attend a War Council at 10 Downing Street. Before I entered the Cabinet Chamber the Prime Minister's secretary, Mr Bonham Carter, beckoned me into his room and jerked out something about the *Hampshire* [...] some suppressed emotion rendered his speech scarcely articulate.
>
> When I entered the Cabinet Room I found the Prime Minister, Sir Edward Grey, Mr Balfour and Sir Maurice Hankey sitting at the table all stunned by the tragedy. One realised how deep was the impression made by the personality of this extraordinary man on all who came in contact with him.

Lloyd George and Hankey quite forgot in their shocked state that it was only the Irish negotiations that had saved them from sharing Kitchener's fate.

Asquith immediately asked Lloyd George to take over at the War Office, but for some time he demurred. 'I had no liking for the prospect of finding myself a mere ornamental figurehead in Whitehall.' Since the appointment of Robertson as CIGS, much of Kitchener's supreme control of the war effort had been delegated, Lloyd George himself being one of those responsible for this state of affairs. Dissatisfied with war direction, and now asked to assume responsibility for it, Lloyd George was thinking of resigning and working in Opposition, but was persuaded not to by Bonar Law.

Perhaps the most fitting eulogy for Kitchener was penned by that rapscallion bounder, journalist-cum-soldier-cum-politician and scion of the ducal house of Marlborough, whom the Field Marshal really could not abide but did his best to be polite to. Churchill wrote:

> The solemn days when he stood forth as the Constable of Britain beneath whose arm her untrained people braced themselves for war, were ended. His life of duty could only reach its consummation in a warrior's death [...] Let us hope they will remember the comfort his character and personality gave his countrymen in their hours of hardest trial.

It was almost an echo of his own subsequent role.

Churchill's re-entry into Westminster had not been a brilliant success. Although he spoke eloquently and frequently, he was still regarded as a failed politician. The likelihood that Lloyd George would go to the War Office occurred to him right away and, without modesty, he hurried round to see his old friend on the day Kitchener's death was announced. 'I suppose you have come after Lloyd George's job,' Lord Northcliffe joked when he saw Churchill there. Churchill stayed for five hours, lobbying hard and finally extracting an agreement from Lloyd George that he would be the best man to succeed him at Munitions, and that he would push it with the Prime Minister. However, the latter thought otherwise. 'Winston's mind is concentrated on the war,' suggested one advocate. 'Yes,' replied Lloyd George, smiling, 'but it is more concentrated on Winston.'

It was a full month before Lloyd George accepted the War Office, and the following five months were the least happy of his career. General Robertson would brook no interference from a civilian chief and plans for an all-out offensive on the Somme were going ahead, despite Lloyd George's serious misgivings. He managed to get the Quartermaster General, Sir John Cowans, 'the most capable soldier thrown up by this war', to help sort out the muddle created by the cumbrous mismanagement of the Indian Army in Mesopotamia, where they were fighting the Turks. It was now too late to do much for Russia, and Lloyd George's cunning plan to get Robertson out of the way by sending him on a mission there failed. His greatest success in this period was to appoint an expert on light railways, Sir Eric Geddes, to start reorganising the Army's supply system in France.

At seven o'clock on the morning of 1 July 1916, whistles blew all the way down the British line and khaki-clad men rose steel-helmeted, gas-masked and with bayonet tips gleaming cold steel on their long Lee-Enfield rifles. Seven days of artillery bombardment had preceded this moment, against an enemy that were well prepared, dug in, ready and waiting at the strongest point on their entire front.

As the hurricane of British shells ceased, a German eyewitness noted:

Our machine guns were pulled out of the dugouts and hurriedly placed into position. A series of extended lines of British infantry were seen moving forward from the British trenches. The first line seemed to extend without end to right and left.

A barrage of rifle and machine-gun fire tore into the advancing soldiers; many flung their arms into the air and fell, never to move again, while others crawled into shell holes.

The noise of battle became indescribable. The shouting of orders and the shrill British cheers as they charged forward could be heard above the violent and intense fusillade of machine guns and rifles and the bursting bombs, and above the deep thunderings of the artillery and the shell explosions. With all this were mingled the moans and groans of the wounded, the cries for help and the last screams of death. Again and again the extended lines of British infantry broke against the German defence like waves against a cliff, only to be beaten back. It was an amazing spectacle of unexampled gallantry, courage and bull-dog determination on both sides.

In places along the 45-kilometre front attacked by British and French forces German trenches were captured, but many could not be held and by nightfall nearly 60,000 British soldiers, the flower of Kitchener's citizen army and some of the best that Britain had ever known, were lying in the churned earth—dead, wounded, or prisoners of the Germans. 'This was the greatest loss and slaughter sustained in a single day in the whole history of the British Army,' commented Churchill.

The German 27th Division at the Somme experienced 'a culminating point ... which was never again approached ... In the Somme fighting of 1916 there was a spirit of heroism which was never again found.' Captain Von Hentig stated plainly, 'The Somme was the muddy grave of the German field army and of the faith in the infallibility of the German leadership, dug by British industry and its shells.'

To disguise the initial failure, Haig ordered the attack to continue in a scaled-down form and strict censorship was initiated in order to keep the real situation from the general public. Lloyd George toured the battlefront behind the lines while the deafening bombardment and 'keen' of flying shells continued from batteries nearby, drowning out conversation. He saw a long line of the Guards Division marching to the attack:

> But before I reached Ypres I heard that the attack had failed and that the brilliant son of the British Prime Minister [Raymond Asquith] was among the fallen.
>
> When I ventured to express to Generals Joffre and Haig my doubts as to whether cavalry could ever operate successfully on a front bristling for miles behind with barbed wire and machine guns, both generals fell ecstatically on me, and Joffre in particular explained that he expected the French cavalry to ride through the broken German lines on his front the following morning. Just then a press photographer snapped us. The conversation gave me an idea of the exaltation produced in brave men by a battle. They were quite incapable of looking beyond, around or through the struggle just in front of them.

On 1 August, a month after the slaughter began, Churchill submitted a memorandum to the Cabinet in which he critically set out the position and argued cogently against the continued massacre of the best men the Allies had merely for trifling gains in ground of little strategic value. For this he was pilloried in the Northcliffe press as 'a failed megalomaniac politician' responsible for the Gallipoli disaster, who now wanted to interfere with the generals' sublime plans for victory. He wrote:

Through this awful arena all the divisions of the army, battered ceaselessly by the enveloping artillery, were made to pass in succession [...] for month after month the gallant divisions of heroic human beings were torn to pieces in this terrible rotation.

A handful of the new tanks were thrown into the battlefield, their novelty bringing isolated but unsupported successes. 'The objectives were now pulverized villages and blasted woods.' The men floundered through mud and slime as the weather broke. In the sky aircraft directed the artillery's targeting and dropped bombs on ammunition dumps, shooting down enemy planes and raiding their airfields while the enemy replied in kind. During late September the battle flared up again. In one instance a single tank supported by two companies of infantry cleared 1,500 yards of German trench, capturing eight officers and 362 men for the loss of only five British soldiers. 'To achieve this miniature success, a secret of war, which, well used, would have procured a world-shaking victory in 1917, [when there were sufficient tanks] had been recklessly revealed to the enemy,' thundered Churchill, who with Lloyd George's encouragement had begged Asquith to prevent the futile and premature revelation of the new weapon. Lloyd George had also lobbied General Robertson, but all he got was the laconic answer, 'Haig wants them.'

Churchill described it thus:

A young army, but the finest we have ever marshalled. The flower of that generous manhood which quitted peaceful civilian life in every kind of workaday occupation, which came at the call of Britain and at the call of humanity and came from the most remote parts of her Empire, was shorn away for ever in 1916.

The Official History of the Great War states:

For this disastrous loss of the finest manhood of the United Kingdom and Ireland there was only a small gain of ground to show [...] never again was the spirit or quality of the officers or men so high, or the state of training, leading and above all discipline of the new British Armies in France so good. The losses sustained were not only heavy but irreplaceable.

Over 419,000 fell in the fight.

'It is claimed that the Battle of the Somme destroyed the old German Army by killing off its best officers and men,' said Lloyd George. 'It killed off far more of our best and the French best.'

Typical of the many volunteers of that lost generation—inspired by idealistic patriotism and humanitarian appeal, and buried in the mud of Flanders—was Pte 11983 Allan Cliffe of the Duke of Wellington's West Riding Regiment. An apprentice engineer, a skilled occupation, Allan was still eager to volunteer at Milnsbridge, Huddersfield, aged 19. He was a keen rugby player, a game popular in the regiment's recruiting area in the mill towns of the West Riding, and encouraged in the battalion. After training, his first deployment overseas was in the Balkans and at Gallipoli. In France he retrained as a machine gunner and took part in the Northern Division's attack towards the redoubts at Thiepval Ridge on 28 September 1916, in which Lieutenant Tolkien, the author of *The Lord of the Rings*, was a junior officer. Very intense and confused fighting took place in the complex of trenches below the redoubts where gas, smoke bombs and tanks were used. The strong points fell, but Allan, aged just 21, was killed. His remains were never found and he is named on the Thiepval Memorial, pier and face 6A and 6B, along with the names of 72,000 soldiers who died on the Somme and have no known grave. New life renews all—his nephew, my father, was born on Allan's birthday, 9 December 1916, and was also named Allan. Private Cliffe won no medals and no eulogies were written for him, except by his own family, but like most soldiers in the Great War, he took his place in the struggle and did his duty. His father and brother also served in the Army and survived.

Over a million men on both sides fell on the Somme battlefields between 1 July and 18 November 1916. A despairing memorandum by Lord Lansdowne, the former Foreign Secretary who had brokered the Entente Cordiale in 1904, asked that if stalemate had now been achieved, what should be done about it?:

> What does the prolongation of the war mean? Our own casualties already amount to one million one hundred thousand. We have had fifteen thousand officers killed not including those who are missing [...] We are slowly but surely killing off the best of the male population of these islands [...] The financial burden is being added to at the rate of £5 million a day. Generations will have to come and go before the country recovers from the loss which it has sustained.

Asked to comment, the High Command truculently repudiated the idea of a stalemate. Both Sir William Robertson and Sir Douglas Haig stolidly expressed their confidence that 1917 would bring victory on the Western Front.

# 10

# The Wizard Takes Charge

By November the offensive on the Somme stood revealed as a staggering fiasco, and everywhere the war seemed to be going badly. Sir Maurice Hankey, the Cabinet Secretary, described feeling like a 'squeezed lemon' after recording the proceedings of several 'really dreadful' meetings of the War Committee. Asquith admitted to a friend that he was 'heartily sick of it'.

An Allied conference in Paris was clouded with pessimism, and as Hankey and Lloyd George strolled the Paris streets after the final session while the exhausted Asquith took a nap back at their hotel, Lloyd George told Hankey of his determination to resign from the government. Hankey tried to dissuade him. 'You ought to insist on a small War Committee being set up for the day-to-day conduct of the war. The chairman must be a man of unimpaired energy and great driving power.' Impressed with the possibilities, Lloyd George wired immediately to arrange a meeting with the Conservative leader Bonar Law. Initially, Bonar Law was dubious, seeing it as a scheme to give the hustling Welshman power by the back door, but Bonar Law was unstable in his own party and was being attacked by Edward Carson's supporters for backing Asquith in the role of war leader for which, in their opinion, he was increasingly unsuited.

At first, the meetings with a tired Asquith to discuss the proposal seemed on the verge of success, particularly after Hankey had explained the background to the Prime Minister as a way of lightening his burden. However, an ill-timed article in Northcliffe's newspaper *The Times* wrecked this by describing Asquith's exclusion from the proposed three-man committee as being 'on the ground of temperament'. This article, inspired by Carson, who hated Asquith, infuriated the Prime Minister, who withdrew his previous agreement. Lloyd George then threatened to resign, but on Tuesday 5 December Asquith himself tendered his resignation to the King, calculating that the others would not be able to form an alternative ministry. He was wrong.

A conference was held at Buckingham Palace the next day at which all the leading protagonists declared they were willing to serve under Arthur Balfour, a previous Prime Minister—all except Asquith, who egotistically declared, 'What is the proposal? That I who have held first place for eight years should be asked to take a secondary position?' The political juggling that followed saw Bonar Law first try to form a coalition, and having failed, advise the reluctant King to send for Lloyd George.

On the previous evening, Churchill had dined with Max Aitken MP, a confidant of both Lloyd George and Bonar Law, and along with the Attorney General F. E. Smith they eagerly discussed the likely composition of a new government. Aitken, who knew more than the others, told Churchill he would have friends in the new administration. 'What!' exclaimed Churchill. 'Aren't I to be in the Government?' Aitken's reply, in a careful form of words he had been asked to use, alerted Churchill to the awful truth. 'Smith,' said Churchill, 'this man knows that I am not to be in the Government!' According to Aitken (later Lord Beaverbrook) Churchill's mood swung from bubbling optimism to blazing anger. 'He abused me most violently, picked up his hat and coat and without even putting them on, dashed into the street. Smith ran after him and tried to calm him but in vain.'

The next day Lloyd George went to the Palace in his best frock-coat and told the King that he would try to form a government. 'I saw him directly he returned and he looked very pale and said he would like to run away to the mountains,' wrote his mistress and secretary, Frances Stevenson. 'I'm not at all sure I can do it,' he said, 'it is a very big task.' But he set about the job with energy and skill.

Although 136 Liberal MPs agreed to back his new government, Liberal ministers from the Asquith administration were openly contemptuous of him forming a successful and long-lived ministry. Only two of them, Edwin Montagu and Winston Churchill, assured him of their support, although the first declined to serve immediately and the second was prevented by opposition from the Tory would-be ministers. Chief among these was Bonar Law, who when asked by Lloyd George if he would rather have 'Churchill for us or against us?' replied, 'I would rather have him against us every time.' The renegade Churchill had never been forgiven by his ex-Conservative colleagues for deserting them and attacking with vigour and witty scorn his old principles. Although the findings of the Dardanelles Commission would do much to vindicate Churchill's role in the Gallipoli débâcle, his fall from grace was used as an instrument of punishment for rank treason to their party.

Lloyd George discussed Churchill's gifts, shortcomings and mistakes, with a view to persuading them of his suitability for office. But they were adamantly against him. Lloyd George wrote years afterwards:

> Here was their explanation. His mind was a powerful machine, but there lay hidden in its material or make up some obscure defect which prevented it always running true […] when the mechanism went wrong, its very power made the action disastrous, not only to himself but to the causes in which he was engaged and the men with whom he was co-operating.

Lloyd George won over the Labour leaders to support his ministry after a lengthy discussion about the war and his future policy, as it affected labour relations. Their leader, Arthur Henderson, agreed to take a post in the new five-man War Cabinet. Having persuaded Arthur Balfour to become his Foreign Secretary, Lloyd George met four other leading Tory grandees—Curzon, Cecil, Chamberlain and Long—and having assured them that both Churchill and the press baron Northcliffe would be excluded from the ministry, he obtained their support. He told Frances Stevenson, 'I shall be Prime Minister by seven o'clock!'

> I resolved to set up a Cabinet of five to whom the whole control of the War should be entrusted [...] it must consist of men who were free from all departmental cares and who could devote the whole of their time and thought to the momentous questions which were involved in the successful direction of a world war.

One exception to this rule was Bonar Law, who became both Chancellor of the Exchequer and Leader of the House, effectively Deputy Prime Minister, as Lloyd George spent less time there than his predecessors in the day-to-day running of the House of Commons.

Disgruntled ex-Liberal ministers watched the formation of the new administration with mixed feelings. They had tied their colours to the mast of Asquithian loyalty and followed his patrician lead of benevolent neutrality—their public stance being one of patriotic restraint. Haldane described his old friend Asquith as 'a first class head of a deliberative council, versed in precedents, acting on principles'. Lloyd George, on the other hand, 'cares nothing for precedents and knows no principles, but he has fire in his belly and that is what we want'.

Churchill was devastated at having been left out of the government. He told Lord Riddell, who was acting as a go-between for Lloyd George, 'His conscience will tell him what he ought to do.' But Lloyd George had no intention of jeopardising his fledgling ministry by pandering to Churchill's notions of decency in politics! He would have to wait, and though Churchill remained surprisingly quiet in public, he carped a great deal behind closed doors to anyone who would listen.

The new government was almost immediately presented with two separate peace notes. One from Berlin and the second from President Woodrow Wilson of the United States. The first was stated in the usual blustering tone of Teutonic arrogance, without offering anything tangible, and the second was a model of public-spirited helpfulness, offering mediation. The new Prime Minister made a statement to Parliament on 19 December:

> Any man or set of men who wantonly or without sufficient cause prolonged a terrible conflict like this would have on their soul a crime that oceans could not cleanse. On the other hand it is equally true that [if we] out of a sense of weariness or despair abandoned the struggle without achieving the high purpose for which we entered into it [we would] have been guilty of the costliest act of poltroonery ever perpetrated by any statesman.

The Allies therefore replied jointly to both notes, rejecting the German demands and thanking the American President in courteous terms for his offer, which created a favourable public opinion on the other side of the Atlantic. Since the loss of the *Lusitania* to a torpedo fired by a U-boat in 1915, America had been increasingly incensed against Germany.

The Germans were not too worried. They demonstrated what they thought would be the clincher when they unveiled their new ocean-going cruiser submarine by sinking five ships within American territorial waters, resulting in further American loss of life within sight of the Nantucket lighthouse. Now they compounded their mistake by unleashing a vastly increased submarine fleet at the end of January 1917, declaring unrestricted submarine warfare on all shipping proceeding to and from Allied ports, to be sunk on sight without warning. They calculated that six months of this would bring the Allies to their knees, starved of supplies, and frighten the Americans into acquiescence. Even if America came into the war, they reasoned, by the time its troops were trained and ready there would be no ships to carry them to Europe! Germany was a young nation and behaved as if run by technically skilful but diplomatically inept teenagers, whose courage was in inverse proportion to their lack of wisdom. This was the final throw of the dice by the German Admiralty and, as little could presently be expected from their army on the decisive Western Front, the last strategic gamble of the war.

Meanwhile, the new Prime Minister was setting his house in order. His daughter Olwen recalled:

> Moving was a simple matter—we walked in from next door [No. 11], by the garden gate. I loved living in No. 10 for there was always something going on. Famous people came and went, and No. 10 seemed to be the hub of the universe.

One day, General Smuts came to tell them that Lloyd George and three guests were coming up for lunch. The general was downcast by high casualty figures that had just been received. Olwen wrote, 'Then there was a noise, and father arrived in a great rush, as he always did.' General Smuts smiled, 'We can't be depressed for long with this man around!'

The Lloyd George family occupied the whole of No. 10, unlike today when the premier has a private flat at the top of the house. So Lloyd George created what became the 'Garden Suburb'—a series of annexe offices out the back, where his special advisers transacted business with a secretariat of their own. His household, including the catering, was organised by Mrs Lloyd George herself, with a Welsh housekeeper and cook. It became for the first time in its history a good solid, frugal, lower middle class establishment. Lloyd George went to bed early and rose early. Before 8 a.m. he had read his official papers and digested the day's news. He then held political meetings over breakfast, much to the distress of Colonel Hankey and colleagues who kept more conventional hours.

The War Cabinet was in continual session. Lloyd George could consult Bonar Law at any time by strolling next door to bounce ideas off the dour Scottish-Canadian businessman, now ensconced as Chancellor of the Exchequer in No. 11. Hyper-efficient Hankey was head of the Cabinet Office, and minutes of decisions were taken, sent to departments and followed up to ensure that action was carried out. He was also secretary of the Committee of Imperial Defence and became a formidable force in Lloyd George's centre-out style of dictatorial government. But Lloyd George, having no intention of being swallowed whole by a single bureaucrat, appointed the economist Thomas Jones as Hankey's chief assistant. Hankey was suspicious of Jones, a former Fabian socialist 'with a sly Welsh face like Lloyd George' in Hankey's opinion. The two balanced one another out. The War Cabinet was now at the core of a vast plethora of committees and conferences of ministers, military men, civil servants and experts of all kinds. At the centre of the web, all the twitching silken threads came back into the hands of one man of prodigious energy and enterprise—Lloyd George.

Churchill, watching from the sidelines, was itching to be part of it. The disasters of 1917 came fast upon one another. First, the mounting submarine threat with record numbers of sinkings, then Lloyd George's premature attempt to foist a French supreme commander, General Nivelle, the hero of Verdun, on the British High Command. Then in March the long-anticipated revolution in Russia, expected to be a simple *coup d'état*, turned into a messy civil war, paralysing the Eastern Front and releasing German reinforcements for the West. Churchill wrote:

It was in facing with unquailing eye these awful contingencies during the opening months of his prime responsibility, that Mr Lloyd George's greatest service to his countrymen will be found to reside. Not only undaunted in the face of peril, but roused by each deepening manifestation to fresh energy, he drove the engine of State forward at increasing speed.

The new Prime Minister possessed two characteristics which were in harmony with this period of convulsion. First, a power of living in the present, without taking short views. Every day for him was filled with the hope and the impulse of a fresh beginning. He surveyed the problems of each morning with an eye unobstructed by preconceived opinions, past utterances, or previous disappointments and defeats [...] his intuition fitted the crisis better than the logical reasoning of more rigid minds.

Mr Lloyd George in this period seemed to have a peculiar power of drawing from misfortune itself the means of future success [...] All parts of the task of government claimed his attention and interest. He lived solely for his work and was never oppressed by it. He gave every decision when it was required. He scarcely ever seemed to bend under the burden. To his native adroitness in managing men and committees he now added a high sense of proportion in war policy and a power of delving to the root of unfamiliar things.

Churchill was bitterly disappointed to find no sphere of action 'in a Ministry with whose aims and temper I was in the most complete accord'. However, his opportunity to help and to rehabilitate himself came sooner than he thought, although Lloyd George was still fearful that using Churchill might bring disaster on his new government. 'Winston is like a chauffeur who drives for months without trouble, then suddenly takes you over a cliff,' he confided privately.

For Lloyd George there were personal disasters also. When he became Prime Minister his doting Uncle Lloyd, now ailing and in his eighties, declared solemnly, 'The man is greater than his office.' In February, the old man who had been such an influence on David as a boy, teaching him independence of thought and manner, a revered pastor and president of the Llanystumdwy village parliament, died at the age of 83. Although his family and some Welsh servants were still around him, the ties with North Wales were loosening fast. Lloyd George found consolation in the arms of Frances Stevenson, and her flat in central London became his alternative home, free of the many stresses of war leadership for a few hours.

He had not been so personally distressed since his favourite elder daughter, his beloved and beautiful Mair, had died of appendicitis at the age of seventeen, ten years before. Since that time his relations with Margaret Lloyd George had cooled considerably, though they still maintained a loving family atmosphere before their children. He had written to his wife at the time:

> I have a profound conviction that, cruel as the blow may appear, and purposeless as it may now seem, it will prove to be the greatest blessing that has befallen us and through us multitudes whom God has sent me to give a helping hand out of misery and worry a myriad worse than ours. I can see through the darkness a ray of hope.

Which, coming from a man who distrusted the existence of God, sounds like sanctimonious egoism,  but it was written for his wife, whose faith was simple and sincere.

The demands of office were relentless, and Lloyd George backed the wrong horse when he threw his political weight behind the plans of Nivelle, who had replaced Joffre. Nivelle, a good talker who appealed to Lloyd George, believed in the concept of hitting the enemy at his strongest point. He attacked in April, supported by the British, at Arras. When he was still losing men but had not broken through by May, he was replaced in turn by General Pétain, who quelled a mutiny in the French Army with a promise there would be no more suicidal large-scale attacks against concrete, machine guns and barbed wire. At Arras the British and Commonwealth troops had made significant gains in ground, capturing Vimy Ridge and advancing for the first time behind a creeping artillery barrage just in front of the soldiers. Miners from New Zealand and Durham had also made miles of tunnels through the chalk bedrock, enabling many men to advance unseen to within yards of the German lines.

Lloyd George had some luck with the Navy at home, when after months of fruitless badgering he forced the Admirals to accept a convoy system to protect ships crossing the Atlantic and other seas. Jellicoe was now First Sea Lord, having handed over the Grand Fleet to Beatty, the dashing commander of the 5th Battlecruiser Squadron that had delivered the German High Seas Fleet to Jellicoe's guns at Jutland. Jellicoe had not been a decisive success in battle and now he proved a brake on the Admiralty. Carson, the First Lord, in Churchill's old job, could get nowhere with him. When Lloyd George questioned him about the U-boat threat, Jellicoe calmly handed over a list of shipping lost. 'I was fairly astounded,' said Lloyd George. Over 900,000 tons had been destroyed in April alone. 'Is there no solution for the problem?' Jellicoe's reply was not encouraging. 'Absolutely none that we can see now.'

Fortunately, younger officers with experience of the problem had some solutions. Commanders Henderson and Kenworthy both believed a convoy system could work. Another Teutonic diplomatic blunder brought the Americans into the war in April, after the Germans had incautiously encouraged Mexico to form an offensive alliance with them against the United States for the invasion of Texas, Arizona and New Mexico! This meant that American ships would now be available and the Royal Navy found it had enough vessels to provide escorts for convoys. At last the Admirals had been persuaded 'not perhaps to take action, but to try action' said Lloyd George wryly. Very quickly the convoy system made a significant difference.

The numbers of ships sunk dropped dramatically, as U-boats had grave difficulties when attacked by escorting destroyers with depth charges and gunfire. The Prime Minister's other great innovation on the seas was the appointment of a Shipping Controller, Sir Joseph Maclay, an experienced ship owner, to make the best use of available ships and to organise their routeing. All this treading on toes and pushing noses out of joint, as the Welsh Wizard eased himself into the driving seat and set scores of mechanics to tune up the engine of government, built up a body of indignation and criticism against Lloyd George's dictatorial style.

To quell the criticism and explain government policy, Churchill suggested a secret session of the House of Commons. Lloyd George, who had been too busy to take much notice of Churchill, accepted the idea and, on 10 May, Churchill opened the debate. In a masterful outline of the situation he described how the Russian Army of seven million men 'has been crushed by the German hammer'. On the other hand, a nation of 120 million of 'active educated and wealthy citizens, commanding intact and almost limitless resources of every kind, has engaged itself in our cause'. He felt sure that Great Britain and America would carry the day, even if 'every [other] ally fails', warning of the peril on the seas and setting out the strategy to pursue for victory:

> Master the U-boat attack, bring over the American millions, and meanwhile maintain an active defensive on the Western Front, so as to economise French and British lives, and so as to train, increase and perfect our armies and our methods for a decisive effort in a later year.

He implored the Prime Minister for the present, 'to prevent the French and British High Commands from dragging each other into fresh bloody and disastrous adventures'.

It was one of Churchill's most successful speeches and the members listened spellbound. But he only narrowly avoided repeating the same gaff that had spoiled his earlier speech when he had called for the return of Fisher to the Admiralty. Fortunately, his suggestion that Asquith be invited to join the government was expunged from the final draft after his cousin, Capt. Freddie Guest, the Chief Whip, ran it past Lloyd George beforehand. The suggestion was equally unwelcome to both Asquith and Lloyd George, and would have merely ruined a good speech.

Lloyd George rose to answer Churchill and began to outline the problems that had faced the government since he had become Prime Minister and how he had dealt with them one by one. Churchill wrote:

> He proceeded to lead a captivated assembly over the whole scene of the war, gaining the sympathy and conviction of his hearers at every stage. When he sat down, the position of the government was stronger than it had been at any previous moment during his administration.

Lloyd George and Churchill met 'fortuitously' behind the Speaker's chair at the conclusion of a debate highly satisfactory to both of them, and, as Roy Jenkins says, 'post-successful-oratorical-bonhomie is a well-known experience to all politicians'. Lloyd George enthusiastically assured Churchill that he wanted him by his side, and quickly arranged for him to have a week's fact-finding tour in France. Frances Stevenson noted in her diary soon afterwards:

> He says he wants someone who will cheer him up and help & encourage him & who will not be continually coming to him with a long face and telling him that everything is going wrong. At present he says he has to carry the whole of his colleagues on his back [...] I think D. [David] is thinking of getting Winston in some capacity. He has an intense admiration for his cleverness, & at any rate he is energetic and forceful.

Others were less impressed by Churchill's gifts. Lord Esher wrote to Field Marshal Haig at St Omer, to warn him of Churchill's impending visit:

> He handles great subjects in rhythmic language and quickly becomes enslaved by his own phrases. He deceives himself into the belief that he takes broad views, when his mind is fixed upon a comparatively small aspect of the question.

But that was merely Esher's opinion, a man who had taken an equally critical view of Kitchener when talking to Churchill and Lloyd George behind the great man's back. Both the Prime Minister and the House of Commons were equally and keenly impressed by Churchill's reinstatement of himself as a front-rank politician.

In June, the remarkable and hideous experiment of Messines Ridge took place when nineteen carefully mined subterranean caverns packed with high explosives were detonated under the German lines. The explosions were heard clearly in Downing Street and, it was claimed, as far away as Dublin. In a few seconds, 10,000 human beings were torn to shreds and scattered over a wide area, buried beneath tons of earth and rock and the detritus of war. Sandbags, gun emplacements, dugouts and trenches all disappeared. As the commander of the operation, General Plumer, had predicted, 'Gentlemen, we may not make history, but we will certainly change the geography.' It did not make much difference to the course of the war, however, as the German reserves poured into defences, and soon Lloyd George was under pressure to agree to another massive offensive near Ypres to capture the Passchendaele Ridge. Keeping up pressure on the Germans, who were unaware that the French troops were in revolt, was essential according to Haig and Robertson, until the Americans could arrive and fill the gap.

Lloyd George had rather cleverly detached Northcliffe from his mischief-making in the press by sending him to head the British Mission in the United States, where he met influential politicians, businessmen and financiers who were all enthusiastic to help but appalled at the $50 million a day price tag. The press baron's brash and can-do attitude was just what was needed and galvanised the staff there, making them less stuffy and British, which the Americans appreciated. So he was absent when Lloyd George sprang his long-contemplated bombshell of resurrecting Churchill in government. Northcliffe hated Churchill, but he was too busy to notice or object when the irrepressible bad boy of politics bounced back.

Others who did notice and were not consulted were appalled. Bonar Law, number two in the government, when told by his friend Max Aitken, was so indignant he let his pipe go out, an unheard-of lapse. 'Lloyd George's throne will shake,' he predicted. But apart from deputations and protests, the attitude of senior Conservatives was one of disgruntled acceptance. In the end, Bonar Law told them that the Prime Minister had every right to make any appointment he chose.

Lloyd George offered Churchill the Ministry of Munitions or the newly constituted Air Board. The amalgamation of the Naval and Army flying services into the RAF was just about to occur with the formation of an Air Ministry, and there was much to be done in developing air defences, aircraft manufacture and offensive deployment. For years, German aircraft, bombers and Zeppelins had made sorties across Britain in an effort to draw away air forces from the front lines, where they were decisive in reconnaissance and attack. Raids over London caused thousands from the East End to seek refuge in Tube stations away from the carnage near the docks, and parks were black with them on summer evenings.

Churchill chose Munitions, Lloyd George's baby. The two men dined together at Downing Street, and after the meal Lloyd George took Churchill through into another room and showed him a framed *Daily Express* placard from the time of the Marconi affair. It said, 'Churchill defends Lloyd George.' The debt was now paid.

# 11

# At the Eleventh Hour

'War is a game to be played with a smiling face,' Churchill had told his officers and men at the front in 1915. Now his smiling face, his energy and his perseverance were needed more than ever by his colleagues in the life-or-death struggle. They were particularly welcome to Lloyd George as he grappled with a variety of bewildering problems, calling for every ounce of resource at his disposal. 'I can only hope that the PM is right in thinking that Winston has taken to heart his error and that he will not use his new position to meddle with the armies or with war policy,' senior Conservative Austen Chamberlain confided to Walter Long. That, of course, was hoping for too much. Churchill continued to bombard Lloyd George with unsolicited strategic advice, much of it absorbed if not acted upon, and the two men were in broad agreement on many objectives. To begin with, Churchill got down to the business of reorganising the chaotic improvisations he found at the Ministry of Munitions, to turn it into an efficient, soldierly machine.

About 12,000 civil servants and businessmen in fifty separate departments were housed in hotels near Trafalgar Square. Churchill at first faced hostility from his officials, but quickly dispelled this by joking about his own unpopularity. He had been quite surprised on regaining office to discover just how deep seated the prejudice against him had become among front-line politicians, but the commander-in-chief Sir Douglas Haig was confident in his abilities as a minister, writing, 'I have no doubt that Winston means to do his utmost to provide the Army with all it requires.' He was less confident of his other tendencies, however:

> He can hardly help meddling in the larger questions of strategy and tactics; for the solution of the latter he has no real training, and his agile mind is a danger because he can persuade Lloyd George to adopt and carry out the most idiotic policy.

Churchill got on with what he was supposed to do. A ministry official, Walter Layton, wrote:

> Lloyd George's flair brought the colossal Ministry of Munitions to life, and had for the first time awakened and harnessed Britain's industrial strength to an all-out war effort.

Winston Churchill's special contribution was to bring discipline and organisation to the Ministry [...] Winston harnessed men into a disciplined team which he then drove.

He regrouped the fifty departments into ten large units, each with its own head, and formed a council of the leaders. Once this was up and running, congestion was relieved. Churchill wrote:

> I was no longer oppressed by heaps of bulky files. Every one of my ten councillors could give decisions in his own sphere [...] Instead of struggling through the jungle on foot I rode comfortably on an elephant whose trunk could pick up a pin or uproot a tree with equal ease, and from whose back a wide scene lay open.
>
> At the Ministry of Munitions I worked with incomparably the largest and most powerful staff in my experience. Here were gathered the finest business brains of the country working with might and main and with disinterested loyalty for the common cause [...] they resigned altogether the immense fortunes which must have come to them had they continued as private contractors. They served the State for honour alone.

But Churchill's warnings not to get bogged down in more premature offensives were not heeded by the government. Lloyd George did not feel himself strong enough to resist the combined arguments of Haig and Robertson and many politicians. Even General Smuts, the former Boer leader, now a special adviser who had been asked to look at aerial defences against bombing raids around London, believed that a summer offensive on the Western Front should take place.

'Ministers were told confidentially that the offensive was urged by the French as the only means of saving France from collapse,' claimed Lloyd George. Years later, after the death of Earl Haig (as the former commander-in-chief became), Lloyd George wrote that the French generals had actually condemned the planned offensive as being doomed to failure and wanted the British Army instead to take over more of their line and remain on the defensive until the Americans arrived in force. But Lloyd George did not know this, as Haig and Robertson had concealed the information. Various detailed objections were mustered against what was to be known as the Third Battle of Ypres or more commonly Passchendaele. The chosen battlefield was a reclaimed swamp, maintained by an intricate system of drainage ditches, continually swept clear by Flemish peasant farmers. Both artillery and tank corps officers objected that this would turn into a quagmire under any barrage. Commanding generals in the field also expressed misgivings, the weather prospects looked bleak, and only GHQ were hopeful of success.

Lloyd George excused himself:

> Profound though my apprehensions of failure were, I was a layman and in matters of military strategy did not possess the knowledge and training that would justify me in overriding soldiers of such standing and experience. Accordingly the 'soldiers' had their way.

After a bombardment which lasted sixteen days—twice as long as the preliminary to the Somme battle—and the inevitable German artillery reply, an observer wrote:

> [...] the ground consisted of nothing but a series of overlapping shell craters, half full of yellow slimy water. Through falling into these ponds hundreds upon hundreds of unwounded men, while advancing to the attack, lost their lives by drowning.

Thirty British and four French divisions attacked along the Ypres salient on 31 July 1917. If they were successful, a supporting amphibious landing was to take place on the coast to destroy the submarine bases in the Belgian ports further north and threaten the Germans in their exposed coastal flank. Churchill wrote:

> Soon the rain descended and the vast crater fields became a sea of choking foetid mud in which men, animals and tanks floundered and perished hopelessly. The few tracks which alone could be preserved across this morass were swept with ceaseless shell fire, through which endless columns of transport marched with fortitude all night long.

Pte Walter Williamson took part in the attack on day one, with the 6th Cheshires, and after a wearying scramble their initial objective of St Julien was behind them. They were scattered, bogged down, shelled and machine gunned to a standstill, and even the tanks sent to help were only a burden:

> They ambled about and one loomed over our strong point [a shell hole] before it toppled nose downwards into the great hole, the caterpillar tracks churning up the ground and making a clank that nearly drowned the noise of bursting shells. It finished up by bursting flame and smoke out of every hole in it, as the crew dashed out.

After a night of pouring rain, Walter and a few others made it back to the start point and were detailed for stretcher-bearing.

> Here a padre in a soaked surplice over muddy uniform was giving a short service over a great open trench, where men who had given their all lay side by side. At one end of the trench lay stocks of equipment muddied and torn, and piles of boots, while an officer busied himself with 'effects'—that cold little word which covers all the intimate treasures found in a soldiers pockets, photographs of home folks, and usually the last letter written home, which had missed the last post.

On the afternoon of day three, the battalion paraded on top of their trench: fifty-seven all told of those who took part in the attack, including three officers and a sergeant major—500 men and twenty officers failed to return. Their experience was multiplied by every battalion that took part.

The battle was renewed with reserves, Lloyd George visiting GHQ in late September. 'I found there an atmosphere of unmistakable exultation. It was not put on. Haig was not an actor. He was radiant. There was no swagger. That was never one of his weaknesses.' General Charteris, his head of military intelligence, also 'glowed with victory'. Lloyd George continued:

> He could not help his hopeful reports. His computations were not mathematical but temperamental. From the mass of information which came into his office he chose his facts and figures by attraction and not reflection. He could only be caught by a bright fly. That he swallowed up to the gut. It naturally pleased Haig to have carefully chosen and nicely cooked little titbits of 'intelligence' about broken German divisions, heavy German casualties and diminishing German morale served up to him every day and all day. He beamed satisfaction and confidence.

GHQ also attempted to mislead its VIP visitors by showing them a specially selected batch of 'weedy' prisoners in order to prove that German resources were at the last gasp.

What Lloyd George did not know was that the field commander, General Gough, had advised Haig to abandon the attack by mid-August. Gough wrote:

> I informed the C. in C. that tactical success was not possible, or would be too costly under such conditions [...] I had many talks with Haig during these days and repeated this opinion frequently, but he told me that the attack must be continued.

Later, Lloyd George wrote:

> It is a comment on the intelligence with which the whole plan had been conceived [...] that masses of cavalry were intended to thunder across this impassable bog to complete the route of a fleeing enemy. For months, hundreds of thousands of British troops fought through this slough. They sheltered and they slept in mud-holes. When they squelched along they were shot down into the slush; if wounded they were drowned in the slime; but the survivors still crept and dragged onward for four months from shell hole to shell hole, with their rifles and machine guns choked with Flemish ooze, advancing about a mile a month. It was a tragedy of heroic endurance enacted in mud.

He condemned the ineptitude of GHQ:

> They lavished the lives placed at their disposal in foolish frontal attacks on impregnable lines [...] They then sent home requisitions for more units [...] Most of the gaps in our manhood were rent by clumsy and unintelligent craftsmanship at the top [...] The Passchendaele fiasco imperilled the chances of final victory.

Yet Charteris knew the truth. In his diary entry for 10 August he records: 'The Front area now baffles description ... it is just a sea of mud, churned up by shellfire.' A young staff officer from GHQ visited the battle front after four months of battle. 'Good God, did we really send men to fight in that?' he cried when he saw the desolate morass, and burst into tears.

The battle was castigated by the war poet Siegfried Sassoon as 'a sepulchre of crime'. Even Haig in his war memoirs admitted it was a mistake—and if not his own, who else's? Lloyd George called eminent military experts Sir John French and Sir Henry Wilson into counsel as independent advisers during October and both recommended a cessation of the offensive. One last throw brought a shaft of hope. Incensed at the futile wastage of their men and machines in the Flanders mud, the tank corps commanders drew up a plan to attack in force on the well-drained chalky uplands around Cambrai further south but received very grudging support from GHQ for the attempt. Led in person by Gen. Hugh Elles in a tank called 'Hilda', 378 tanks crashed through no man's land at dawn on 20 November, without the giveaway barrage beforehand. By nightfall they had advanced further than all the fighting of the previous three months had achieved. However, because they were not supported by adequate reserves to follow up the tanks and secure the ground, the Germans, after the initial surprise, had plenty of time to counter-attack. The premature ringing of victory bells in London was followed by the loss of even more ground.

The War Cabinet was angry and, smelling blood, demanded of Robertson, the CIGS, what was to be done. He attributed the mistakes of Third Ypres primarily to the over-optimistic intelligence reports of General Charteris and deficiencies in planning the attack to General Kiggell, Haig's chief of staff. He was also inclined to blame General Gough, the field commander for 'persisting in the attacks after it had become evident that they could not succeed'. So everyone except the main author was to be chastised. The War Secretary, Lord Derby, and Robertson were immediately sent to France to demand that Haig sack these three generals. For obvious reasons, Haig refused to dismiss Gough (it might have proved awkward if he had revealed the truth), instead moving him and his army to what he hoped would be a rest and recuperation sector further south. Lloyd George considered that Robertson, as the professional head of the Army, had signally failed to advise the Cabinet of the true situation in Flanders, but both he and Haig still enjoyed widespread support in the press, the House of Commons and among many influential Conservatives in the government. To remove them was a tricky proposition, and at that stage it was difficult to see who might successfully replace Haig. Unimaginative and under-inspired he might be, but he was the best they then had. Colonel Hankey and General Smuts were sent by Lloyd George to tour the Army, talent spotting, but came back glum and empty handed. 'In the grand army that fought the World War the ablest brains did not climb to the top of the stairs, and they did not reach a height where politicians could even see them,' he wrote.

Frances Stevenson noted in her diary on 6 November, 'D. has made up his mind that General Robertson has got to have his power taken away from him.' Lloyd George wrote of the tricky situation, 'I never believed in costly frontal attacks either in war or politics, if there was a way round. In this case I sought and found one, which in the end achieved the purpose.' Meanwhile, the Italian Army had collapsed in the face of Austrian and German attacks in northern Italy, and British divisions had to be rushed through France and via railway tunnels under the Alps to bolster them up. Also in October, the Bolsheviks overthrew the liberal government in Russia, quickly signing the peace treaty of Brest-Litovsk, which released colossal numbers of German troops for deployment on the decisive Western Front. The British and French armies were exhausted and hung grimly on the defensive, awaiting the arrival of the hoped-for vigorous young American troops.

An Allied conference at Rapallo in Italy provided the opportunity to discuss the creation of a Supreme Allied War Council. It received unanimous agreement, and even President Wilson said that the United States would be happy to allow the use of its troops under such an arrangement. It gave Lloyd George the opportunity to outmanoeuvre Robertson by offering him the post of military representative on the Council at Versailles, or to remain as CIGS at the War Office with reduced powers. He accepted neither, and it came down to a trial of strength.

In the meantime, the King had agreed to the removal of Jellicoe as First Sea Lord, following his inability to work with the dynamic new First Lord, Sir Eric Geddes. Jellicoe had suffered from a virtual paralysis of decision-making, as if he felt that doing nothing would be safer than making a wrong choice. Geddes, having sorted out the transport system behind the lines in France to the great satisfaction of Haig, was now charged by Lloyd George to go through the Navy like a dose of salts. He discovered that the main blockage sat in Admiralty House. Jellicoe had opposed the convoy system, which was proving its worth by rapidly overcoming the U-boat threat, and the discredited admiral had to go. On Boxing Day 1917 he was forced to resign. 'He will not be missed,' was Lloyd George's only comment.

Turning to his battle with Robertson, Lloyd George was determined, but far from sanguine. He told his adviser Philip Kerr, 'We may be packing our bags in a week.' But he decided, even if the government fell, to carry on his freelance fight against what he perceived as military bungling. A heavy cold laid him low for a couple of weeks just as the intensity of press and political opposition reached its peak. A succession of colleagues came to argue the case for retaining Robertson, and finally there was a debate of confidence in the House of Commons. Lloyd George lucidly outlined the situation, concluding:

If the House of Commons tonight repudiates the policy for which I am responsible, and on which I believe the saving of this country depends, I shall quit office with but one regret—that is, that I have not had greater strength and greater ability to place at the disposal of my native land in the gravest hour of its danger.

The press were mollified by his explanations, the Opposition cowed; Haig stood aloof from the controversy, and Robertson resigned as CIGS to take up the Eastern Command, a theatre of war in which he had little interest and where most of the hard fighting had been done. He was replaced as CIGS by Gen. Sir Henry Wilson, an articulate and idiosyncratic Irishman of high intelligence. Lloyd George had won this battle, but the war was far from over.

Churchill had been busy with his work at Munitions during all this controversy. His farmhouse home at Lullenden in Surrey, where Clemmie and his growing family of four children were safely ensconced from the air raids over London, was a convenient staging-post for flights to a château near GHQ in France, kindly provided for him by Haig, where he could see everyone he needed to. Churchill spent much time in France, which he loved. He wrote to Clemmie from Paris, 'You really must find some excuse to come for a few days to this ever delightful city.' Churchill then viewed the preparations for a great defensive battle expected soon:

> Very different was the state of the line from what I had known it to be when serving with the Guards in 1915 or as a battalion commander in 1916 [...] Contact with the enemy was only maintained through a fringe of outposts.

Drawn back from these were killing zones—avenues of barbed wire interspersed with machine-gun nests—beyond that, batteries of field guns well dug in, and beyond that, battalion HQ and the heavy batteries. 'For four miles in depth the front was a labyrinth of wire and scientifically sited machine-gun nests. The troops though thin on the ground were disposed so as to secure full value from every man.'

A brooding silence fell across the front. 'The sunlit fields were instinct with foreboding,' wrote Churchill graphically. He visited South African troops in Gauche Wood. 'I see them now, serene as the Spartans of Leonidas on the eve of Thermopylae.' In the early hours at Divisional HQ he awoke to complete silence and lay there musing:

> Suddenly, the silence was broken by six or seven very loud and heavy explosions several miles away [...] and then, exactly as a pianist runs his hands across the keyboard from treble to bass, there rose in less than one minute the most tremendous cannonade I shall ever hear [...] Far away, both to the north and to the south, the intense roar and reverberation rolled upwards to us, while through the chinks in the carefully papered window the flame of the bombardment lit like flickering firelight my tiny cabin.

Churchill dressed and went outside where he met the divisional general Sir Henry Tudor on the duckboards. 'This is it,' he said. 'I have ordered all our batteries to open. You will hear them in a minute.' But the crash of German shells exploding a few hundred yards away was so tremendous that the much closer firing of 200 guns was blotted out.

One could see the front line for many miles. It swept around us in a wide curve of red leaping flame [...] and quite unending in either direction [...] the enormous explosion of shells upon our trenches seemed almost to touch each other with hardly an interval in space or time [...] the weight and intensity of the bombardment surpassed anything which anyone had ever known before.

This was the great German attack of 21 March 1918. The barrage did not last long before German troops loomed through the grey early-morning mist, amid the chatter of machine guns and the bursting of hand grenades, and quickly outran the front-line outposts. These were a new breed of soldier—the storm troopers—hand-picked, battle-hardened men of athletic physique, equipped with all the latest hand-portable weaponry and trained to bypass centres of resistance which could be mopped up by follow-on troops. Gas shells deliberately rained on the rear areas, disrupting communication and cutting off the front line from reinforcement. Worse, the British front had now been extended by twenty-five miles to cover a previously French-held sector and reserves were low. Churchill was persuaded by his travelling companion, the Duke of Westminster, that they had better get out while the going was good. A captive (or dead) Minister of Munitions would be of no use to the war effort.

On arrival in London, Churchill went straight to the War Office where he met the new CIGS, General Wilson, wearing a grave face, surveying his maps and reading the latest telegrams from France. Together they walked across to Downing Street. Churchill recalled:

It was a bright crisp day. Mr Lloyd George was seated in the garden with Lord French. He seemed to think that I had news at first hand and turned towards me. I explained [...] that I had seen nothing except the first few hours of bombardment in a single sector.

Lloyd George took him on one side and asked how positions further back could be held with already defeated troops when the most carefully fortified ones had been easily overrun? Churchill explained in layman's terms that an attack was like throwing a bucket of water over the floor. At first, it rushed forward, then soaked forward and finally stopped altogether until another bucket could be brought. 'After thirty or forty miles there would certainly come a considerable breathing space, when the front could be reconstituted.'

That evening, Lloyd George, Wilson and Churchill dined together at Churchill's house in Eccleston Square. Churchill reassured Wilson that even if a thousand guns had been lost, they and all the ammunition could be replaced from the Ministry of Munitions' reserve supplies. 'I never remember in the whole course of the War a more anxious evening,' recalled Churchill. But he continued:

One of the great qualities in Mr Lloyd George was his power of obliterating the past and concentrating his whole being upon meeting the new situation. There were

200,000 troops in England that could be swiftly sent [...] The resolution of the Prime Minister was unshaken under his truly awful responsibilities.

General Wilson departed to catch his train for France, and the two men were left together to plan and plot for an unknown future.

Churchill was sent by the Prime Minister as a special envoy to General Foch, soon to become the Supreme Allied Commander. Wilson, on being told of Churchill's mission, thought it unwise as it breached military protocol, and Churchill received a wire telling him to visit Clemenceau, the new French Premier, first. As usual, however, he pleased himself, careering about the front, but he did go and see The Tiger, as the 76-year-old veteran Clemenceau was known—because he savaged almost everyone who crossed his path! He had been given his chance when France was desperate for a leader who could make something out of a desperate situation. Rather like Churchill in 1940, the old man was a political gamble, and, just like with Churchill, incredibly, it worked. As a young man, Clemenceau had seen Paris in flames under the Prussian bombardment of 1871, and now he burned with indignation and determination to punish 'The Boche' for again invading his beloved France.

'Five military motorcars all decorated with the small satin tricolours of the highest authority filled the courtyard,' remembered Churchill. Clemenceau advanced upon the British Minister of Munitions with a greeting in slightly Gallic English:

> I am delighted my dear Mr Winston Churchill that you have come. We shall show you everything [...] We shall see Foch. We shall see Debeney. We shall see the Corps commanders, and we will also go and see the illustrious Haig and Rawlinson as well. Whatever is known you shall know.

First, they received a briefing from Foch, dramatic in its intensity, 'during which every muscle and fibre of the General's being seemed to vibrate with excitement and passion'. This ended with Clemenceau hugging the general in a Gallic embrace. Moving on, the cavalcade reached General Rawlinson's HQ, where he was rebuilding the shattered remnants of Gough's 5th Army into his own 4th Army. Field Marshal Haig joined them for lunch and implored the French Premier to send reinforcements to strengthen the critical sector of the British front. Clemenceau, having agreed, demanded the 'reward' of going forward into the battle zone.

Writing to Clemmie of the experience, Churchill noted:

> He is an extraordinary character. Every word he says—particularly general observations on life and morals—is worth listening to. His spirit and energy indomitable. 15 hours yesterday over rough roads at high speed in motor cars. I was tired out—& he is 76!

Churchill compared him to Fisher—'[He is] just as ready to turn round and bite! I shall be very wary.' The greatest achievement of Churchill's visit was to persuade

Clemenceau to join Lloyd George in an appeal to President Wilson to speed up the transfer of American forces to France.

While the desperate battles continued, with the German hammer blow falling repeatedly first against the British then the French, and the storm troop technique flooding past defences, Lloyd George found himself attacked closer to home. General Maurice, former director of military operations at the War Office, claimed in the press that Lloyd George and Bonar Law had deliberately starved the British Army in France of reinforcements earlier in the year, after Passchendaele, and were therefore partially responsible for the defeats that followed. A debate threatened to overwhelm the government in May, but Lloyd George, on form with his brief, quoted Maurice's own statistics provided by his deputy at the War Office, which showed that the strength of the Army was greater in January 1918 than a year earlier. Later (when it no longer mattered), it was found that the figures supplied were probably wrong, but by then the danger had passed. It seems likely from the evidence that there was a conspiracy to discredit the government by supplying misleading figures to the Prime Minister in the first place.

Lloyd George called for unity. 'I really implore, for our common country, the fate of which is in the balance now and in the next few weeks, that there should be an end to this sniping.' Maurice was dealt with for his serious breach of discipline by the military authorities, who let him off lightly by placing him on retired pay.

When the emergency in France was at its height, Marshal Foch was offered the Supreme Allied Command on the recommendation of Haig himself. 'It is a hard task you offer me now,' responded Foch, 'a compromised situation, a crumbling front, an adverse battle in full progress. Nevertheless I accept.' Lloyd George's dream of a united command was thus achieved in the moment of extremity. The British and French soldiers disputed every yard of ground in close fighting that never ceased, day or night. The German losses in attacking were at least double those of the defenders. Young drafts from England were thrown into the battle before they knew their officers or one another. Haig, now a field marshal, issued his famous 'backs to the wall' order of the day:

> There is no other course open to us but to fight it out. Every position must be held to the last man. There must be no retirement. With our backs to the wall and believing in the justice of our cause, each one of us must fight on to the end.

With only the Channel ports behind them, there was no room for manoeuvre.

Although he deplored the earlier disasters on the Somme and at Passchendaele, Churchill was moved to telegraph to Haig, 'I cannot resist sending you a message of sympathy and sincere admiration for the magnificent defence which you are making day after day, and of profound confidence in the result.' Numberless small contingents of men continued to fight, until, cut off and overwhelmed, they were blotted out. By the end of April the BEF had lost a quarter of its strength, but the

Germans had lost far more. 'The sense of grappling with a monster of seemingly unfathomable strength—invulnerable since slaughter even on the greatest scale was no deterrent—could not be excluded from the mind,' wrote Churchill. No one expected a swift result. The British public were resigned to a long struggle.

Churchill was also grappling with labour relations in the munitions factories, where skilled workers were objecting to the piecework rates of the unskilled that often exceeded their wages. Strikes all over the country disrupted production. Coventry proved particularly difficult to appease, but the threat of suspension of reserved status and conscription for strikers, coupled with intimidation by members of the National Sailors' and Firemen's Union, and hectoring from Miss Christabel Pankhurst, got them back to work. Churchill also had a 'give them the money' attitude to the workers and little sympathy for the profiteering factory owners, which helped.

From his Munitions headquarters in France, 'an old French country house amid wonderful avenues of trees near the village of Verchocq', Churchill toured the battlefront:

> One way or another I managed to be present at almost every important battle during the rest of the war. Once I flew in a fighting plane between the lines while a considerable action was in progress below [...] But from the height of 7,000 feet to which we had to keep on account of the German artillery, there was nothing to see but the bursting shells of the barrages far below. It is impossible to see a modern battle. One is either much too far or much too near.

For Germany, things were taking a sinister turn. Its allies, Turkey, Bulgaria and the Austro-Hungarian Empire, were gloomily desperate for peace; a mutiny disrupted the smooth functioning of the German Navy; even the valiant German Army became infected with Bolshevik ideas, and desertions increased. The people, short of food, began to despair. America was now pouring troops into France at the rate of a quarter of a million men a month, fresh and eager for the fray. While German soldiers were eating coarse rye bread and husbanding resources, the Allies waxed fat and their arsenals clanged day and night at full production, pouring forth munitions of war. Implements of destruction and supplies of every kind converged on France in endless convoys of shipping. Now, at last, had come the turning of the tide.

At 8 a.m. on a summer morning in the deep forest near Soissons on the flank of a violent German storm trooper drive across the River Marne, 350 small and well-hidden Renault tanks were revving their engines in anticipation of a sudden swoop into the open country below. Behind and around them were French and American infantry divisions in overwhelming numbers. The Germans had advanced so far that they had stopped to harvest the abundant corn. As the fighting machines clanked out of the woods, the German soldiers cast down their sickles, grabbed their rifles and fought where they stood. The high corn hampered their deployment of machine guns as the tanks ploughed murderously through their ranks, decimating and scything the defenders from the field. Survivors were driven back five kilometres. Churchill commented:

> The decisive blow on the Western Front had not yet been struck; but from this moment onwards to the end of the war, without exception, the Allies continued to advance and the Germans to retreat. Unseen upon the surface, the turn of the tide had now begun.

A further attack by British and Dominion soldiers under General Rawlinson, led by 600 tanks, smashed through the barbed wire, deep trenches and dugouts of the Siegfried Line on 8 August, aided by mist and smoke. In less than two hours 16,000 prisoners and 200 guns were taken, and by midday tanks, armoured cars and even British cavalry were scouring the country up to ten miles behind the German line. Churchill eagerly flew to the scene of battle.

> I was much delayed in reaching it by enormous columns of German prisoners which endlessly streamed along the dusty roads [...] The woebegone expression of the officers contrasted sharply with the almost cheerful countenance of the rank and file.

Lloyd George wrote:

> The Germans, not without reason, thought they had made that line impregnable. Even the troops who overran it could hardly understand their own achievement when they examined afterwards in cold blood the defences they had stormed: immense tank-proof trenches, sunken fields filled with barbed-wire entanglements, strong points and machine-gun nests and vast shell-proof dugouts and underground chambers where whole battalions could shelter from a barrage.

After seeing Rawlinson at HQ, Churchill set off by car on a battlefield tour:

> [...] through deserted, battered, ghostly Amiens; through Villers-Bretonneux, a heap of smouldering wreckage, threading our way through an endless convoy which moved slowly forward from one shell-hammered point to another. The battlefield had all its tales to tell. The German dead lay everywhere, but scattered in twos and threes and half dozens over a very wide area. Rigid in their machine-gun nests, white flaccid corpses, lay those faithful legionaries of the Kaiser who had tried to stem the rout of 'six battle-worthy German divisions'. A British war balloon burst overhead into a sheet of fire from which tiny black figures fell in parachutes. Cavalry cantered as gaily over the reconquered territory as if they were themselves the cause of victory. By a small wood, seven or eight tanks with scattered German dead around them lay where a concealed battery had pierced them, twisted and scorched by the fierce petrol fires in which they had perished.

Experiences like these led Churchill to the view that the British were playing a predominant part in the victorious push forward. He differed from Lloyd George, who increasingly ascribed the success to unity of command under Foch, but Churchill seriously believed that this was unfair on Haig.

> His armies bore the lion's share in the victorious advance, as they had already borne the brunt of the German assault [...] On more than one cardinal occasion, Haig, by strenuous insistence, deflected the plans of the Supreme Commander with results which were glorious.

Churchill was with Haig when he ordered the simultaneous attack of three British armies at Bapaume. Pointing to the German lines on the map, Haig declared to Churchill, 'Now you will see what all these fortifications are worth when troops are no longer resolved to defend them.'

By 28 September, Ludendorff and Hindenburg simultaneously came to the conclusion that the military situation was hopeless and could not be sustained for long. An immediate armistice, while Germany still held some ground, must be demanded, for Germany had lost 1½ million men between March and the end of September. Ludendorff wrote:

> It is not the low strengths of our divisions which make our position serious but rather the tanks which appear by surprise in ever increasing numbers [...] our operations on the Western Front have now assumed the character of a game of chance.

Churchill was sceptical of the move. 'Those who choose the moment for beginning wars do not always fix the moment for ending them. To ask for an armistice is one thing, to obtain it is another.' A new German Chancellor, Prince Max von Baden, sent a request to Woodrow Wilson accepting the President's previous peace initiative as a basis for agreement. On 24 October, the U-boat campaign was called off and all submarines were ordered to return. Three days later, Ludendorff, who had changed his mind, was dismissed by the Kaiser. On 4 November, the Austro-Hungarian Empire, defeated by the Italian and Allied forces, signed an early armistice. Germany's partners sued for peace and German delegates crossed the Allied lines to negotiate an armistice. Two days later, the Kaiser abdicated and fled to Holland.

On the same day, Lloyd George invited Churchill and Edwin Montagu, the only two senior Liberal ministers in his government, to lunch. Montagu, who had married Asquith's former paramour Venetia Stanley, was a wry observer of what followed. 'Winston began sulky morose and unforthcoming. The Prime Minister put out all his weapons. He addressed him with affection as "old man". He reminded him of their old campaigns.' Winston eventually revealed what he objected to—'the degradation of being a minister without responsibility for policy' outside the tiny

War Cabinet. Lloyd George cheerfully waved these objections aside. The existing arrangement would end with the war, and a new Cabinet of ten or twelve of the most important ministers would be formed. Montagu watched Churchill as 'the sullen look disappeared, smiles wreathed the hungry face, the fish was landed'.

Parliament was told the terms of the intended Armistice—immediate evacuation of invaded countries, repatriation of inhabitants, surrender of all munitions and implements of war, locomotives, vehicles and aeroplanes, most of the German fleet, evacuation of the left bank of the Rhine and bridgeheads, and repatriation of all prisoners of war. 'Overwhelming thankfulness filled all hearts,' Churchill recalled.

A few minutes before the eleventh hour of the eleventh day of the eleventh month, Churchill stood at the window of his office looking towards Trafalgar Square waiting for the chimes of Big Ben to announce that the war was over. The street was deserted.

> Then suddenly the first stroke of the chime. From the portals of one of the large hotels absorbed by the government departments darted the slight figure of a girl clerk, distractedly gesticulating while another stroke of Big Ben resounded. Then from all sides men and women came scurrying into the street. Streams of people poured out of all the buildings. The bells of London began to clash. Northumberland Avenue was now crowded with thousands rushing hither and thither in frantic manner, shouting and screaming with joy. I could see Trafalgar Square was already swarming [...] the tumult grew, it grew like a gale, from all sides simultaneously.

Lloyd George was standing in the gardens behind No. 10 Downing Street with his staff, listening to the throbbing cheers of the crowds. Already planning a general election, he meant to have another four years of power. 'He can be Prime Minister for life if he wants to be!' cried Bonar Law in an uncharacteristic fit of optimism.

Churchill was joined by Clemmie, and together they decided to go and congratulate the Prime Minister in the moment of triumph:

> But no sooner had we entered our car than twenty people mounted upon it and in the midst of a wildly cheering multitude we were impelled slowly forward through Whitehall [...] It was with feelings which do not lend themselves to words that I heard the cheers of the brave people who had borne so much and given all, who had never wavered, who had never lost faith in their country or its destiny and who could be indulgent to the faults of their servants when the hour of deliverance had come ...

# Epilogue

One of the architects of glorious victory lay in a watery grave at the bottom of the North Atlantic Ocean. Kitchener was an enigma and continues to remain so. His reputation was attacked both during his years of power and immediately after his death. He suffers from the censure that First World War generalship received with the benefit of hindsight from subsequent generations of writers—the 'lions led by donkeys' label. Because he could not defend himself, and took no part in the Paris Peace Conference that followed the war, his later career, which could have shone a different light upon his wider qualities, remains hypothetical. He never had the opportunity to write his memoirs and give his side of the story, unlike the other protagonists.

The stern field marshal was the epitome of the military commander so accurately portrayed in the text of Sun-Tzu, written two and a half millennia before Kitchener was born. *The Art of Warfare* states:

> As for the urgent business of the commander: He is calm and remote, correct and disciplined. He is able to blinker the ears and eyes of his officers and men, and to keep the people ignorant. He makes changes in his arrangements and alters his plans, keeping people in the dark. He changes his camp and takes circuitous routes, keeping people from anticipating him.

It was this impenetrable quality that so baffled his political colleagues. Both Lloyd George and Churchill were frustrated and resentful of 'being kept in the dark' and suspected that it was a cover for bungling incompetence. To Kitchener, security and keeping vital military information from civilians was essential. He was always a military man first and a politician second. But the primacy of politics demands that those in government must know and be kept informed of the basis of decisions arrived at by the military chiefs, who are in the role of their advisers.

His former ADC, later Field Marshal Birdwood, wrote of his old chief:

> All his life he was a curiously shy man, except with those he got to know intimately, and I am convinced that this shyness of his was the main cause of the reputation he acquired for being abrupt and brusque. Once this initial reticence had worn off he was entirely approachable.

Birdwood's anecdote of an incident during a garden party at the Viceregal Lodge in India showed a gentler side to Kitchener's personality. Birdwood's son Chris, then a small boy, was frightened by a loud crash and ran to Lord Kitchener, 'seizing his hand and standing close to him for protection'. A year or two later, when Kitchener was asked by his cousin Edith what had been the proudest moment of his career, he replied, 'I think when little Chris ran across and put his hand in mine with such complete confidence.'

Field Marshal Robertson described him as 'easily the most outstanding personality at the Allied Conference. He was listened to with more deference than anyone else … on the whole I would say that the achievement and foresight of Lord Kitchener place him in a class entirely by himself.' The Labour leader Arthur Henderson said that Kitchener was 'entirely free from the spirit of intrigue'. The working men of the country, in their hearts, believed in his word, a more imperishable monument than any in stone.

No one would claim that Churchill or Lloyd George were free from the spirit of intrigue. They were politicians to the bone, and the epithet 'troublemaker' might have been coined for either of them. But in the world crisis their capacity for rocking the boat and interfering with the helmsman eventually made for a happy landfall. Immediately on the cessation of hostilities, Lloyd George cashed in on his current value as 'the man who won the war' by holding a general election. His candidates for a continued coalition government were given coupons of approval to wave at the electorate as bona fide supporters of the war effort. Churchill was one such candidate, and after scuffles with trade union hecklers at his constituency in Dundee was easily re-elected in the landslide result.

He became the new Secretary of State for War and immediately set about the demobilisation of the 3½ million-strong army, with the Cabinet priority of saving money. The war had racked up debts that would take many decades to pay off. But he was also rather keen on the idea of doing something to stem the revolutionary tide in Russia, and a patchwork of British and Allied troops guarding ammunition dumps at Archangel and Murmansk were maintained as a possible nucleus for another military adventure. Not all soldiers wanted to go home, and those addicted to danger and violence also signed on as a paramilitary police force in Ireland known as the 'Black and Tans', and their ex-officer cohort the 'Auxis'. They were supposed to fight the IRA, but largely succeeded in terrorising the entire population, both loyalist and nationalist.

Churchill fired off his memoirs in *The World Crisis* before Lloyd George, but the Welshman had the last word in his *War Memoirs*. His considered assessment was that the generals' idea of a war of attrition was 'the refuge of stupidity' and had resulted in an Allied superiority in men being melted down in four years to the dimensions of a dubious equality:

War is not an exact science like chemistry or mathematics, where it would be a presumption on the part of anyone ignorant of its first rudiments to express an opinion

[...] War is an art, proficiency in which depends more on experience than on study and more on natural aptitude and judgement than on either.

Soldiers might spend a lifetime in barracks without a day's experience of the realities:

> When the Great War broke out our Generals had the most important lessons of their art yet to learn [...] Had they been men of genius, which they were not, they could have adapted themselves more quickly and effectively to the new conditions of war. They were not equipped with that superiority in brains or experience over an amateur steeped in the incidents and needs of the war which would justify the attitude they struck and the note of assured past-mastership they adopted to all criticism or suggestion from outside or below. The Generals themselves were at least four-fifths amateur hampered by the wrong training.

With storm clouds gathering in 1938, Lloyd George wrote in the preface to the second edition of his book:

> The last great struggle revealed not only the squalid and horrid aspects of war but its muddles; its futilities; its chanciness; its wastefulness of lives, the treasure and virtues of mankind—all that demonstrates the supreme stupidity of committing to such a brutal and blunder-headed tribunal as War the determination of issues upon which the happiness and progress of humanity so largely depend.
>
> When all the people that on earth do dwell are gladly scraping the butter off their own and their children's bread in order to keep the god of war fit and sleek, it is necessary to show them clearly what a fool he really is.

Despite Lloyd George's rhetoric, his pyrotechnics, his romantic outlook, he was a most practical statesman, judging men by what they accomplished rather than by rank or reputation. Of Haig he said, 'He was brilliant—brilliant to the top of his boots.' Lloyd George achieved much, but his 'dizzying changes of direction' described by his biographer Jenkins, were more to do with his focus on the present and its practical exigencies than any coherent game plan for the future. Churchill saw things more in the light of history and (preferably) his place in it. Knowing both men well, Lord Beaverbrook (Max Aitken) reckoned that 'Churchill was perhaps the greater man but [Lloyd] George was more fun'. Churchill's humour was carefully prepared, but Lloyd George's strokes of wit were sparked off by the moment as if a sprite had flashed by.

In the late 1920s, long after Lloyd George had ceased to hold office, Churchill, who was now Chancellor of the Exchequer in a Conservative government, sent for him to elucidate some questions for his book on the Great War. The two men were alone for about an hour; then the secretary, Bob Boothby, heard Lloyd George leave.

After ten minutes, he went through and found Churchill in an armchair gazing into the fire. 'How did it go?' he asked.

'You will be glad to know that it couldn't have gone better. He answered all my questions.' Then a hard look came into Churchill's face as he went on, 'Within five minutes the old relationship between us was completely re-established. The relationship between master and servant. And I was the servant.' Boothby, who came to know Churchill well, was later to write, 'Historians a hundred years from now will acclaim Lloyd George as Britain's greatest wartime Prime Minister.' It seems he agreed with Churchill's own early estimate!

Churchill never really did escape the influence of Lloyd George. Even when he became a wartime Prime Minister himself in 1940, he was still hankering after his old political partner and trying to get him into the government in some capacity or other. But for Lloyd George it was too late. Now an old man, he told his private secretary, A. J. Sylvester, 'I'm not going in with this lot; running a department would kill me.' Another reason was that, much as he had always admired Churchill's better qualities, Lloyd George found his 'obstinacy, impulsiveness, conceit and lack of judgement' intolerable in a subordinate, and impossible in a superior.

Let us give Churchill the last word. His eloquence, though flowery, was always a saving grace. To paraphrase, 'He marshalled the English language and sent it out to fight!' Writing of post-Armageddon Europe, as the devastated landscape began gradually to re-emerge with restructured towns and reclaimed countryside during the 1920s, he posed a question that is still relevant for us today, and for all the generations to come:

> New youth is here to claim its rights and the perennial stream flows forward even in the battle zone, as if the tale were all a dream. Is this the end? Is it to be merely a chapter in a cruel and senseless story? Will a new generation in their turn be immolated to square the black accounts of Teuton and Gaul? [...] Is it conceivable that in our own day the hand of destiny will raise the curtain on an even greater horror? [...] Will our children bleed and gasp again in devastated lands? Or will there spring from the very fires of conflict that reconciliation of the three giant combatants [Great Britain, Germany and France], which would unite their genius and secure to each in safety and freedom a share in rebuilding the glory of Europe?

# Bibliography

Ames, Roger T. (ed.), *Sun-Tzu: The Art of Warfare*, Random House, 1993

Asquith, Margot, *More Memories*, Cassell, 1933

Beaverbrook, Lord, *The Decline & Fall of Lloyd George*, Collins, 1963

Bonney, George, *The Battle of Jutland 1916*, The History Press, 2010

Carey Evans, Olwen, *Lloyd George Was My Father*, Gomer Press, 1985

Cassar, George H., *Kitchener: Architect of Victory*, William Kimber, 1977

Churchill, Winston S., *My Early Life*, Odhams Press, 1930

Churchill, Winston S., *The World Crisis 1911–1918*, Thornton Butterworth, 1932

Cross, Colin (ed.), *Life with Lloyd George: The Diary of A. J. Sylvester 1931–45*, Macmillan, 1975

Esher, Viscount, *The Tragedy of Lord Kitchener*, John Murray, 1921

George, William, *My Brother and I*, Eyre & Spottiswoode, 1958

Gilbert, Martin, *Churchill: A Life*, William Heinemann, 1991

Grigg, John, *The Young Lloyd George*, Eyre Methuen, 1975

Grigg, John, *Lloyd George: The People's Champion 1902–1911*, Eyre Methuen, 1978

Grigg, John, *Lloyd George: From Peace to War 1912–1916*, Methuen, 1985

Hankey, Lord, *The Supreme Command 1914–1918*, Allen and Unwin, 1961

Jenkins, Roy, *Asquith*, Collins, 1986

Jenkins, Roy, *The Chancellors*, Macmillan, 1998

Jenkins, Roy, *Churchill*, Macmillan, 2001

Koch, H. W., *The Age of Total Warfare*, Bison Books, 1983

Koss, Stephen, *Asquith*, Allen Lane, 1976

Liddell Hart, Basil, *History of the First World War*, Cassell, 1970

Lloyd George, David, *War Memoirs*, Odhams Press, 1938

Lloyd George, Richard, *Lloyd George*, Frederick Muller, 1960

Longford, Elizabeth, *Wellington*, Weidenfeld & Nicolson, 1992

Longford, Elizabeth, *Winston Churchill*, Book Club Associates, 1974

Messenger, Charles, *The Century of Warfare*, Harper Collins, 1995

Morgan, Kenneth O., *Lloyd George*, Weidenfeld & Nicolson, 1974

Parker, Geoffrey (ed.), *The Times Atlas of World History*, Harper Collins, 1993

Priddey, Doreen (ed.), *A Tommy at Ypres: Walter's War*, Amberley, 2011

Royle, Trevor, *The Kitchener Enigma*, Michael Joseph, 1985

Steevens, G. W., *With Kitchener to Khartum*, Blackwood, 1898

Taylor, A. J. P. (ed.), *Lloyd George: A Diary by Frances Stevenson*, Hutchinson, 1967

Taylor, A. J. P. (ed.), *My Darling Pussy*, Weidenfeld & Nicolson, 1975

Toye, Richard, *Lloyd George & Churchill: Rivals for Greatness*, Macmillan, 2007

Warner, Philip, *Kitchener: The Man Behind the Legend*, Hamish Hamilton, 1985

# Index